Report 178   London, 1998

Sealant joints in the external envelope of buildings

A guide to design, specification and construction

S R Ledbetter BSc PhD CEng MICE

S Hurley BSc PhD

A Sheehan BA (Oxon) MIM CEng

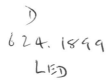

CIRIA *sharing knowledge ■ building best practice*

6 Storey's Gate, Westminster, London SW1P 3AU
TELEPHONE 0171 222 8891   FAX 0171 222 1708
EMAIL switchboard@ciria.org.uk
WEBSITE www.ciria.org.uk

Summary

This report gives guidance for the sealing of joints in the building envelope using sealant systems and sealing strips. The intention is to make designers, specifiers, contractors, specialist subcontractors and suppliers aware of best practice at the design, specification and construction stages.

The topics covered include function and requirements of sealant joints, sealant selection, joint design, construction details and installation. The report emphasises the need for an iterative process of sealant selection, joint design and joint spacing and identifies the role played by different parties in the design and construction teams. Detailed information is provided on:

- causes and magnitudes of movement at sealant joints
- forms of building envelope construction
- performance of generic types of sealant
- selection of sealant systems
- environmental issues
- health and safety issues
- design and spacing of joints
- sealant joints in multi-layered walls
- typical construction details
- site practice

Sealant joints in the external envelope of buildings: a guide to design, specification and construction.

Construction Industry Research and Information Association
Report 178, 1998

© CIRIA 1998, Crown Copyright
ISBN 0-86017-480-8

Construction Industry Research and Information Association
6 Storey's Gate, Westminster, London SW1P 3AU
Telephone: 0171 222 8891   Facsimile: 0171 222 1708
Email: switchboard@ciria.org.uk

Keywords		
Walls, building envelope, joint, cladding, sealant, design, specification.		

Reader interest	Classification	
Design, specification, construction and supervising architects and engineers involved in building construction. Contractors, specialist subcontractors, sealant manufacturers and suppliers.	AVAILABILITY CONTENT STATUS USER	Unrestricted Guidance based on good practice Committee guided Building designers, specifiers, contractors

Acknowledgements

This guide is the result of a research project carried out under contract to CIRIA by a consortium led by Dr S R Ledbetter of the Centre for Window & Cladding Technology, with Dr S Hurley of Taywood Engineering Limited and A Sheehan of Ove Arup & Partners. It provides provides guidance on the design, sealant selection, specification and installation of sealant joints in the external envelope of buildings, complementing and extending other CIRIA reports concerned with joints and seals.

The project was developed and managed by Ann Alderson, research manager at CIRIA, with advice and guidance from a project steering group, whose support and valuable contributions are gratefully acknowledged. The steering group comprised:

Mr Ernest Wakefield *(Chairman)*	Frank Graham, Consulting Engineers
Mr Brian Barnes	Constructive Courses
Mr John Beasley	Building Research Establishment
Mr Cliff Buckton	Sir William Halcrow & Partners Ltd
Mr Bill Dart	Servicised Ltd
Mr Mike Finn	Morton International *representing ASA*
Dr Allan Hutchinson	Oxford Brookes University
Mr Bruce Martin	Bruce Martin Associates *representing the RIBA*
Mr Ian Moffatt	Fosroc Expandite Ltd
Mr Richard Sykes	Wintech Environmental Ltd
Mr Brian Yoxon	Glass and Glazing Federation

The project was funded jointly by Department of the Environment, Construction Directorate, and CIRIA's Core Programme.

Contents

List of Figures

List of Tables

Selective glossary

Adhesive failure	Failure of the joint at the sealant-substrate interface.
Back-up material	Material inserted in a joint that limits the depth of sealant applied and defines the back profile of the sealant.
Bond breaker	Material (e.g., tape or foam) applied to the back of a joint to prevent sealant adhesion.
Butt joint	Joint having opposing faces that may move towards or away from each other.
Cellular sealing strip	Usually a cellular synthetic polymer, which may be impregnated, that is compressed in a joint to effect a seal.
Characteristic tolerances	Expected limits for induced deviations unless particular steps are taken to reduce induced deviations.
Cohesive failure	Failure of the joint within the sealant bead.
Compatibility	The property of a sealant to remain in contact with another material without unfavourable physical or chemical interactions. Compatibility does not imply adhesion.
Compression joint	Joint in which the sealant material is at all times subjected to a positive compressive stress because of a closing tendency of the joint faces, but which is less than that required to squeeze out the sealant so that the faces meet.
Concealed joint	Sealant joint that is not readily accessible from the face of the construction.
Construction joint	Joint between different materials or between stages of construction, not necessarily intended to accommodate movement.
Contraction joint	Joint between building components (e.g., newly cast concrete) where the initial movement resulting from the shrinkage of either or both components is never reversed by subsequent expansion due to other factors.
Cure	Chemical process of hardening or setting, e.g., by chain extension or cross-linking of polymers.
Deviations	Differences between designed and installed dimensions of a joint.
Elastic sealant	Sealant in which the stresses induced in the cured sealant as a result of movement at a joint are almost proportional to strain.
Elasto-plastic sealant	Sealant that has predominantly elastic properties, but exhibits some plastic properties when stressed for other than short periods.

Expansion joint	Joint provided in a structure designed to accommodate expansion and contraction movements.
Failure	The point at which the seal no longer performs the function for which it was installed.
Filler boards	Boards or other material filling the majority of a joint cavity. Often only semi-flexible. Usually also used to form the joint when one structural component is placed or cast against another.
Fillet seal	Triangular section of sealant used to seal a non-moving right-angled joint.
Fixed joint	Joint between components or assemblies that are restrained at, or near to, the joint so that very little movement occurs.
Gasket	Preformed, precured material, forced into a joint to provide a seal.
Induced deviations	Variations resulting from the process of construction.
Inherent deviations	Variations resulting from inherent material properties.
Joint filler	Compressible non-adhesive material used to fill movement joints during their construction.
Lap joint	Joint where there is an overlap of surfaces such that there will be a shear force applied to the sealant in the gap.
Mastic	Compressible material that remains essentially paste-like beneath a surface skin which forms after application.
Modulus	Measurement of the force required to attain a given extension of a material.
Movement	Changes in dimensions or positions of the components to bring about (at joints) relative movement of the boundaries of those components.
Movement accommodation factor (MAF)	Total movement range between the maximum compression and the maximum extension that a sealant can tolerate. It is expressed as a percentage of the minimum joint width (relates to acceptable stress in joints).
Movement joint	Joint designed to accommodate calculated movement.
One-part sealant	Sealant supplied ready for use. (See Two-part sealant)
Open joint	Joint that is not sealed but may prevent passage of water due to the joint geometry.
Permissible deviations	Acceptable limits for induced deviations.
Plastic sealant	Sealant in which the stresses induced as a result of movement at a joint are rapidly relieved.

Plasto-elastic sealant	Sealant that has predominantly plastic properties with some elastic recovery when stressed for short periods.
Polymer	Substance with molecules consisting of one or more structural units repeated any number of times.
Primer	Surface coating to prepare joint faces for application of the sealant.
Sealant	Material, applied to a joint in an uncured state, that seals by adhering to appropriate surfaces in the joint.
Sealant joint	Joint made using either a sealant system or a sealing strip.
Sealant system	System of compatible components – back-up, primer, sealant – that are intended to be used together to form a sealant joint.
Sealed joint	Joint to prevent passage of air or water or both. Joint may be sealed by a gasket or as a sealant joint.
Sealing strip	Preformed material that constitutes a seal when compressed between appropriate joint surfaces and may have adhesive properties.
Sealing tape	See Sealing strip.
Service life	The period of time during which a sealant fulfils its function.
Shear joint	Joint in which one face may move parallel to the other.
Shelf life	The period of time after manufacture when the manufacturer recommends that the material be used. It is affected by conditions of storage.
Solvent-based sealant	A sealant (e.g., an acrylic type) that contains a solvent added by the manufacturer to lower the viscosity of the paste, thus easing application and the ability to 'wet' surfaces. The sealant hardens as the solvent evaporates.
Substrate	Material to which the sealant system or sealing strip is required to adhere to make a sealant joint.
Surface conditioner	'Chemical primer', a reactive chemical that promotes adhesion of the sealant to the substrate.
Tooling	Compaction and smoothing of sealant into joint after application.
Two-part sealant	A sealant supplied as two separate components that have to be mixed before application.
Wetting	A measure of the ease with which a liquid will flow across a surface, penetrating the interstices, without breaking into droplets.
Width:depth ratio	Ratio of sealant width to depth (critical for joint performance).

Abbreviations

AAMA	Architectural Aluminium Manufacturers' Association
ACI	American Concrete Institute
BASA	British Adhesives & Sealants Association
BCSA	British Constructional Steelwork Association
BDA	Brick Development Association
BPF	British Plastics Federation
BRE	Building Research Establishment
BRS	Building Research Station (now BRE)
BS	British Standards
CAD	computer-aided design
CDM	Construction (Design and Management) Regulations 1994
CHIP2	Chemical (Hazard Information and Packaging) Regulations 1994
CIRIA	Construction Industry Research & Information Association
COSHH	Control of Substances Hazardous to Health Regulations 1988
CWCT	Centre for Window & Cladding Technology
DoE	Department of the Environment (now DETR)
DPM	damp-proof membrane
EN	Euronorm
EU	European Union
GFRP	glass-fibre-reinforced plastic
GRC	glass-fibre-reinforced concrete
ISE	Institution of Structural Engineers
ISO	International Standards Organisation
MAF	movement accommodation factor
PVC-U	unplasticised polyvinylchloride
SCI	Steel Construction Institute
SERC	Science & Engineering Research Council (now EPSRC)
UV	ultraviolet

Introduction

Scope and purpose of the document

The objective of this CIRIA guide is to promote good practice and better understanding for the use of sealants in the building envelope. There are few new buildings that do not, in some part, depend on sealant joints to prevent the ingress of air or water. On the largest projects, the sealant joints may extend to tens of kilometres, yet the cost of sealant joints is still low in comparison to the total project costs. For this reason insufficient attention is often given to the design and construction of the joints and preventable premature failure too often occurs. The cost of premature failure can be several times greater than the initial cost of the joints. Sealant joints can be designed and constructed to achieve a service life of 25 years or more. However, some buildings have required resealing within five years.

Sealed joints have traditionally been made using mortars and grouts, mastics and putties. Today joints are sealed using sealant systems, either wet-applied sealants based on polysulfides, polyurethanes, silicones and acrylics, preformed cellular sealing strips such as neoprene or sealant strips based on synthetic polymers such as PVC and polyethylene. It is the use of these sealant systems and the design and construction of the joints in which they are used in the building envelope that form the subject of this guide.

The construction of durable joints that match the performance criteria required for the building can only be achieved by good design, good specification and good installation. This guide covers not only design and specification of sealant joints but also considers the appropriateness of different design solutions. The quality of construction and sealant application required to achieve the intended performance is also considered.

A sealant joint comprises two major elements: the gap into which the sealant system is placed and the sealant system itself. The performance of a joint is dependent on both and may be significantly reduced by the use of either an inappropriate sealant system or an incorrect gap detail. The gap consists of a void and two surfaces to which the sealant adheres. Half of all sealant joint failures are due to adhesive failure between the sealant and the substrate. This document gives guidance on the location of joints, geometry of joints, the suitability of different sealant systems and the requirements for their specification and application.

For the purpose of this guide, sealant system includes wet-applied sealants and cellular sealing strips.

Joints may also be closed by the use of dry gaskets and by mortars and grouts. However the construction of such joints and the design and specification of gaskets is not covered in this guide.

Open joints are frequently used in multi-layer walls. These walls comprise a rainscreen, in which the joints are not sealed, and a back wall, which is sealed to prevent excessive air leakage. This document shows the use of sealants to seal joints in the air barriers of multi-layer walls. It does not cover the detailed design of open joints.

The sealing of trafficked areas such as balconies, walkways and areas for rooftop parking, which have very different performance requirements, are not covered in this guide.

DESIGN RESPONSIBILITY

On any construction project many decisions will influence the design of sealed joints. It is important that all decision-makers understand the consequences of their actions as they affect the sealing of the building envelope. The design, and ultimately the performance, of sealant joints will be affected by the architect, structural engineer, building services engineer, main contractor and subcontractor.

The CDM (Construction Design and Management) Regulations require everyone involved in design to avoid foreseeable health and safety risks (Section 3.1.6).

The architect makes decisions on the general arrangement of the facade, which often dictates the joint spacing and locations, and selects the materials to be used as frames and panels on the façade, which determines the substrates to be joined and thermal and moisture movements.

The structural engineer makes decisions on the structural system for the building and the support system for the building envelope, which determine the movements of the structure and the facade.

As structural movements are normally the largest experienced at any sealant joint, the structural engineer should play an important part in sealant joint design.

The building services engineer makes decisions on the type, size and location of vents and ducts passing through the building envelope. On some buildings this may be the most demanding use of sealant joints. Wherever possible, such penetrations should be minimised.

The main contractor plans the construction sequence and controls site conditions. The main contractor may preclude the use of some forms of sealant joint by setting short timescales for the installation of sealants or by setting particular health and safety requirements. Main contractors can have a detrimental effect on the performance of sealant joints by changing specifications or permitting the use of materials other than those specified.

The specialist subcontractor may make a valuable input to design if he and the sealant supplier are consulted at an early stage. They can advise on suitability of materials, joint spacing and design and, above all, the constructability of the joint.

On any job, one person should be given responsibility for the design and specification of sealant joints. It may be the architect, the structural engineer or a specialist designer/specifier. That person should have an overview of joint design and should consult with all those who may in some way influence the design and performance of the joint. It is important that the joint designer is identified at an early stage as the design of joints is time consuming. Early identification of the joint designer allows time for the necessary collaboration with all the parties and a proper resource can be allocated within the design and construction costs.

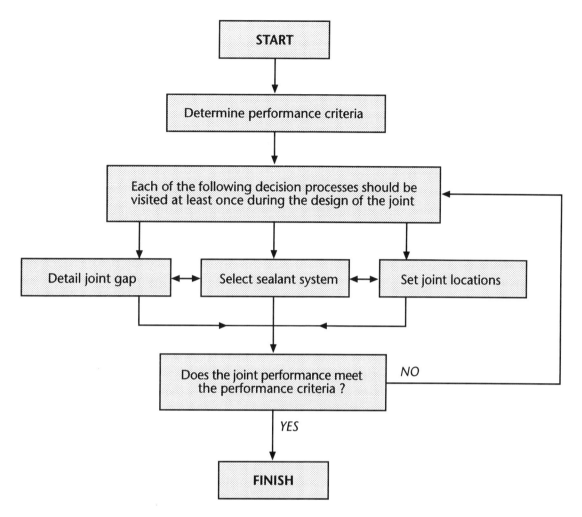

Figure 1 *Decision-making process for design of a sealant joint*

Note: the design of a sealant joint can start with any one of the three design processes: detail joint gap, select sealant system or set joint locations, but all three must be considered at least once.

STRUCTURE OF THE GUIDE

This guide is structured to match the sequence of processes shown in Figure 1. First, it deals with the function and the location of joints and performance criteria in **Section 1: The function, requirements and building components of sealant joints**.

It next deals with joint design. **Section 2: Materials used to seal joints** describes the selection of an appropriate sealant system; **Section 3: Principles of design of joints with sealants** describes the design of joint gaps and joint spacing; **Section 4: Construction details** shows how sealant joints are incorporated into the building envelope. Finally, the report describes good site practice in **Section 5: Installation**.

The reader, in considering the design, performance and construction of joints, may consult any one section of this guide at a time but should always be aware that the design of joints must take account of all of the aspects covered here and is likely to be an iterative process. *There has to be an overall strategy for the design and evaluation of performance for sealant joints*, as set out above.

1   Function, requirements and building components of sealed joints

1.1   GENERAL

The envelope of a building moderates the internal environment of the building and acts as a filter between the external environment and the internal environment. The wall or roof has to have openings for ventilation of the building, draining and ventilation of cavities in the wall, access, passage of light and so forth. Traditional buildings of brick or stone absorb water and dry out, often have high thermal mass and change temperature gradually, and often leak air in an uncontrolled manner to give ventilation. In comparison, modern engineered facades may consist of traditional materials used in a non-traditional way, but also of impermeable materials such as metals, plastics and glass. These are usually installed in large panels or sheets and place a greater demand on the sealing technology required to create a watertight envelope that breathes. This guide deals with the design of joints in the external envelope and the use of wet-applied sealants or cellular sealing strips to provide a water and/or air seal.

1.1.1   What is a joint?

BS6100 defines a joint as a 'Construction formed by the adjacent parts of two or more products, components or assemblies when these are put together, fixed or united with or without the use of a jointing product'. A joint in the building envelope may be defined as any discontinuity in the fabric located in a pre-determined position between either similar or dissimilar materials.

Joints must accommodate tolerances in the design and manufacture of components and their assembly, and tolerances of elements constructed in-situ.

Joints must be capable of accommodating all repeated movements occurring after installation, including thermal and moisture movements and movements of the primary structure due to wind and other imposed loads.

Joints must accommodate single movements that occur at the time of construction and subsequently as a result of shrinkage, settlement or deflection.

Sealant joints must prevent the ingress of water, the leakage of air or both. Their integrity must be maintained throughout their working life under all of the conditions and movements listed above.

Joints may be site-made or factory-made as part of an assembly. In either case the joint will be subjected to the same working environment and should be designed to meet the same performance requirements.

1.1.2   Open and closed joints

A joint may be either open or closed.

Closed joints are sealed with a gasket, a preformed sealant strip or a wet-applied sealant that cures in place. Both gasket and sealant joints provide a continuous barrier to the passage of air and water.

Open joints are not sealed but are left open as gaps between two components of the building envelope. They are not barriers to the passage of air, though air flow can be reduced by providing compartmentalised cavities behind the joints as in a pressure-equalised wall. Open joints will provide a barrier to the passage of rainwater if they are suitably lapped, probably having a labyrinthine geometry. The likelihood of passage of water through open joints is further reduced by pressure equalisation, which reduces the velocity of air flowing through the joint gap.

1.1.3   Movement joints

Movement joints are required in the building envelope to accommodate movement of the components due to thermal and moisture expansion and contraction. They are also required to accommodate movement transmitted from the building structure as a result of floor loading, wind, earthquake, settlement, creep and its thermal expansion and contraction. Floor deflections may induce large movements in the building envelope, particularly where the cladding is attached to the floor edge (Section 1.6).

For large structures with movement joints in the building frame, the movement of the building structure will not be uniform. Differential structural movements will be concentrated in the building frame, and the building envelope will require corresponding movement joints to accommodate the displacements. If cladding elements span across structural movement joints they will tend to rotate.

The location and magnitude of movements depend specifically upon the nature of the cladding attachments and the presence of wind restraints, together with the stiffness of the supporting structural frame and the location of fixings with respect to connections in that frame. For example, large concrete panels will make use of gravity seatings while lightweight panels will be hung; this will give rise to movements associated with such panels either at the top or at the bottom of them, respectively (see also 1.5, 1.5.7–1.5.9, 4.4.1–4.4.6). It is important to consider specific details which require careful attention, such as the junction between mullion and vertical fins, and the influence of the building construction details which may give rise to significant joint movements taking place at particular locations.

Movement joints will also have to accommodate tolerances between adjacent components or assemblies.

Movement joints have been differentiated as expansion joints, contraction joints and compression joints as follows:

Expansion joint: A joint provided in a structure designed to accommodate expansion and contraction movement

Contraction joint: A joint between building components (e.g., newly cast concrete) where the initial movement resulting from the shrinkage of either or both components is never reversed by subsequent expansion due to other factors.

Contraction joints are primarily found in highway pavements, concrete retaining walls and concrete blockwork. They are provided to prevent tensile cracking elsewhere in the construction. Most joints in the building envelope will have to accommodate a whole range of movements, one of which may be initial shrinkage movement.

Compression joint: A joint in which the sealant material is at all times subjected to positive compressive stress, because of a closing tendency of the joint faces, but which is less than that required to squeeze the sealant out of the joint so that the faces meet.

The assumption of permanent compressive stress should be checked by consideration of all the movements at the joint, as many of the joints sealed as part of the building envelope will experience tension.

1.1.4   Fixed joints

Joints may be provided simply to accommodate tolerances between adjacent components and to allow for the assembly of components into a complete element on site. This function may be fulfilled by movement joints, which must be designed to accommodate both movement and tolerance. However it is most convenient to fix joints that are required only to accommodate tolerance. This enables smaller joints to be used and makes different demands on the sealant as a material.

Joints designed as fixed joints with no, or very little, accommodation of movement should have the adjacent components mechanically fixed to ensure that only low movement occurs. This may involve the mechanical fixing of two adjacent framing members or the stitching together of sheeting one sheet to another (Section 3.1.2).

Particular consideration has to be given to the use of adhesive sealants and sealant tapes that provide a seal but also serve to attach two components being joined. In general such a joint will not provide adequate fixity to limit movement and the joint should be designed to accommodate all of the calculated, unrestrained, movement of the components or assemblies. The use of sealants in this way should be limited to the attachment of cover caps, beads and similar small lightweight components.

1.2   SEALANT JOINT DESIGN

Sealant joint performance is determined by the environmental aspects of location, size, geometry, the material of the jointing products used and the substrates to be joined.

1.2.1   Joint design process

There are four principal aspects to joint design:

- understanding what the joint has to do in practice
- selecting and evaluating a sealant system
- setting the joint locations
- detailing a gap.

Any of these aspects may be addressed first to start the design process, but the normal, but not necessarily best, starting point is a consideration of joint locations. However, a joint design will not be optimised unless all of these aspects are visited, probably several times (Figure 1 in the Introduction). The process is an interactive one although good designers will use their knowledge and experience to make a better initial design. Modification of the substrate may allow a better joint and sealant system. Selection of a suitable sealant is described in Section 2. The detailed gap design for joints is described in Section 3. Examples of joint design are given in Section 4.

1.2.2   Joint location

Joint location is often determined by the aesthetics of the facade, by the materials to be used, and by panel or component sizes. In too many cases the detailed joint design is undertaken at a late stage when the designer responsible has little control over the position of the joints. For roofs there is more opportunity for the sheet size and joint spacing to be selected with full regard for the detailed joint design. The early identification of the joint designer and collaboration between him and the architect in determining the joint locations will lead to a better joint design.

The design can rely on a few joints at large spacings that accommodate large movements at each joint, or the movement can be distributed across more joints at smaller spacing, each of which then has to provide for less movement (Sections 3.1.4 and 3.3.5). In general, the use of closer joint spacing will allow the use of narrower joints and although there will be more joints they may be less noticeable.

1.2.3   Shape of sealant joints

The spacing and location of the joints will determine the movement to be accommodated at each one. The joint may be detailed as a butt, lap or fillet joint and the gap may be visible or concealed (Section 3.3.1). The detailing has obvious aesthetic considerations as it will determine the gap width required to accommodate the movement. The use of concealed joints may provide protection from weathering and reduce the rate of degradation of the jointing product but will also have implications at the time of resealing the building (Section 3.5.3). All sealant systems may have to be replaced during the life of the building. Sealants that are accessible may be removed and replaced whereas sealants that are inaccessible will require an alternative approach to resealing. Construction details for different joints are given in Section 4.

1.2.4   Sealant system

For the purpose of this guide, sealant system is taken to include wet-applied sealant systems and cellular sealing strips. The latter are described further in Sections 2.1.2 and 2.2. Wet-applied sealant systems comprise a sealant plus a bond breaker, back-up material and frequently a primer to ensure, among other things, adhesion and placement. The components are described in Section 2.1. Joint design must consider the sealant as part of a sealant system or the intended performance is unlikely to be achieved. Sealants for sealing joints in today's building envelopes are polymer-based, typically polysulfides, polyurethanes, silicones and acrylics. All of these come in a large variety of grades, and the joint designer can opt to use a sealant that offers large movement capability in a small joint, a sealant that offers resistance to degradation in a particular environment and so on. The performance of each sealant material is related to its exact formulation; in general, higher-performance materials cost more.

1.3   SEALANT JOINT PERFORMANCE REQUIREMENTS

Sealant joints must satisfy many requirements but principally they must accommodate movement, provide a weathertight seal and be durable. The sealant joint has to provide a seal throughout its design life and under all combinations of joint movement. Joints in the building envelope are often in highly visible areas of the building facade. It is important that in addition to the technical performance criteria, proper consideration is given to the aesthetics of the joints in the facade.

1.3.1   Appearance

Joints may be either concealed/recessed in the facade or placed prominently on the facade. In the latter case they are likely to be the subject of considerable discussion as to their effect on the overall appearance of the building.

There is a temptation to make joints as narrow as possible to reduce their visual impact and to increase the spacing between the joints for the same reason. This often conflicts with the need to accommodate movement and should be resisted. A full consideration of the joint sizes, joint spacings and sealant systems available might suggest that the building designer's original concept is not achievable and that more joints will have to be visible in the facade.

Attempts to match the sealant colour to that of the substrates in order to reduce the visual impact are seldom successful as an initial colour match is soon lost when dirt accumulates differently on the sealant and substrate; the effects of light and weathering also will vary for each. The use of different but not contrasting colours often gives a better appearance in the long term.

The use of cover plates and flashings to conceal sealant joints may achieve the required aesthetic for the facade. If joints are to be treated in this way proper consideration must be given to the question of resealing and maintenance (Sections 2.11, 3.5.3 and 5.5).

1.3.2   Building and component tolerances

All joints are required to accommodate deviations from target dimensions due to tolerances on manufactured components and their assembly and tolerances allowed in the in-situ construction of building elements (Sections 3.4.4, 3.4.5). Movement joints must also accommodate the calculated movement.

Joints should not be expected to make good greater dimensional deviations arising from poor site workmanship and setting out or gross errors of manufacture and measurement of openings. It must not be assumed that joint dimensions can be changed on site to correct mistakes made elsewhere. Changes to the specified size of a sealant joint should only be made after consultation with the joint designer as it will often be necessary to use a different sealant and/or support for the sealant.

Permissible deviations for windows are given in the British Standards for different framing materials. The Standards generally apply to window frames, but the same deviations can be expected for door frames. Many manufacturers regularly work to closer tolerances. Permissible deviations for curtain walling are given in *Standard for Curtain Walling*, CWCT, 1996. Although most curtain walling is site-assembled, tolerances for plane walls are generally as good as for windows. Permissible deviations of manufactured products are given in Tables 3.6, 3.7 and 3.9.

Deviations on other assembled products may be more significant. This is particularly the case for large elements partially assembled on site and elements of complex geometry such as bay windows, barrel-vault roofs and other forms of roof glazing. Deviations on these assemblies will be different from those normally calculated on the basis of component deviations and may be greatly affected by errors of angular measurement. In these cases appropriate allowances for fit should be made and joints designed accordingly.

For most interfaces between factory-made components and building elements constructed on site the predominant problem with deviations will rest with the site construction, these deviations being up to an order of magnitude greater than factory deviations.

Characteristic tolerances for building construction are given in Table 3.8. These characteristic tolerances, taken from BS5606: 1990, are based on measurements of typical construction. Better tolerances can be achieved routinely by the use of normal good practice methods and use of suitable jigs (Section 3.4.4).

Deviations to be accommodated in joints between on-site construction and prefabricated components can be mitigated by accurate surveying of openings before manufacture of components. This may not be practicable for new-build projects, where lead times are short and the closing of the building envelope lies on the critical path for internal fit-out and completion of the entire building, but they may be an option on a refurbishment project. However, a window manufacturer will want to supply a run of windows at a nominal size to avoid issues of marking and identification of individual windows on site. An accurate survey will establish nominal sizes for components and also show the narrowest and widest joints that will result. This will enable proper design of the joints such that dimensional extremes can be accommodated. This may require alternative joint designs/sealant specifications to be used as appropriate. A proper survey of a window opening should take account of width, height, squareness, plane and line.

1.3.3   Weathertightness

Sealed joints are required to provide a barrier to air leakage and/or water penetration. Sealant systems correctly selected for use in the external sealing of buildings will meet these requirements if they do not deteriorate under use or suffer cohesive or adhesive failure.

Many curtain walling systems, both proprietary and custom-designed, make use of multi-layer sealing. Typically, they have a primary defence of an open joint, gasket or sealant near to the outer face and a secondary seal near to the inner face. In systems of this form the inner seal provides the air barrier and is the predominant control of air leakage through the building envelope. The function of the outer primary seal or open joint is defence against rainwater ingress into the fabric of the envelope, but in the case of an open joint it may not provide a complete barrier. In walls with a front seal only, the primary defence must be airtight and watertight.

Drainage and ventilation

The majority of curtain walls and other components are not front-sealed but have openings in them. These may occur unintentionally at the mitred corners of gasket joints or intentionally as open-lapped joints. Walls of this type are designed as drained and ventilated walls. They are provided with internal drainage routes such that any water that passes the primary defence is drained to the outer face of the wall. The drainage openings also allow air to circulate within the wall between the primary and secondary defences. This reduces the moisture levels within the wall. Drained and ventilated walls are designed to have openings in their outer face and not all of the openings require the attention of a sealant gun. Care must be taken in the use of sealants within the cavities of the wall or within the rebates of frames as these can lead to the blockage of drainage routes. Manufacturers should be consulted if there is any doubt about the appropriate sealing of such systems.

Testing

Facades, and the joints in them, may be tested for watertightness either prior to construction, to assess design, or after installation, to prove design and workmanship. Many curtain walls are tested before construction as full-scale mock-ups of custom curtain walling or as standard test panels of proprietary walling. Any amendments made to details as a result of tests on mock-ups should be documented and care taken that they are actually incorporated into the real project.

Tests include static and dynamic watertightness tests, air permeability tests, thermal regimes and building movement regimes. Similar tests are performed on roof glazing systems. The test programme will prove all joints within the curtain walling system and a curtain wall mock-up will often include interfaces to adjacent components.

Site testing of sealed joints in walling and roofing systems is often undertaken using the hose-pipe test described in AAMA-501-94. However, this may not be an appropriate test in all cases as it is primarily used as a quality test to ensure consistent workmanship, materials and site conditions. If the hose-pipe test shows a joint failure the causes of failure should be examined. If the validity of the hose-pipe test is in doubt it should be verified by comparison with a static watertightness test. Test procedures for curtain walling evaluation, including the hose-pipe test are given in *Standard for Curtain Walling*, CWCT, 1996.

1.3.4   Movement

The movements imposed on sealed joints are of two distinct types: repeated reversible movements and single unidirectional movements. The magnitudes of the movements to be accommodated will depend on the causes described in Section 1.6. The nature of the movement will depend on its cause. A building movement such as creep will give rise to a unidirectional joint movement. Movements due to windloading or thermal movement will be repeated and reversible with frequent cycling. At any joint the movement regime will be due to a combination of causes and may be predominantly reversible or predominantly unidirectional.

Sealants should be selected to match the performance requirements. There are two types of behaviour exhibited by sealants: elastic deformation and plastic deformation. There are four basic classifications for sealants:

- plastic sealants
- elastic sealants
- elasto-plastic sealants
- plasto-elastic sealants.

Full definitions of these sealant performance classes are given in Section 2.7.4.

1.3.5   Fire performance

Fire-resistant sealed joints can be constructed using appropriate protection to isolate the sealant from the fire. For building envelopes, the usual concern is to prevent fire breaking out from within the building. In this case, suitable insulating, fire-resistant material is placed as part of the joint filler and back-up. Note that the joint filler and back-up must still meet all the requirements set out in Section 2.7. The design of fire resistant joints will probably require the advice of a specialist and/or testing of the proposed joint.

Most polysulfides, polyurethanes and silicones may burn, but flame-resistant sealants are available. Such sealants are self-extinguishing. Again, the advice of a specialist should be sought. BS476: Parts 6, 1989 and 7, 1987, give test methods and classification for surface spread of flame.

1.4 SUBSTRATES

Any joint in a building envelope will be between two or more different materials or two components made of the same material – the substrates. The substrates to be joined will have two effects on the performance of the joint. First, they will affect the thermal and moisture movement of the joint (Sections 1.6.1 and 1.6.2). Second, they will affect the interface between the sealant and the substrate. Adhesion between the sealant and a component will depend on the selection of a suitable sealant/primer system for the particular substrate. Half of all sealant joint failures occur as adhesion failures. Problems may also occur from sealant migration into the substrate and consequent staining. Some sealants are incompatible with particular substrates or other sealants. Friable substrates may be weaker than the sealant used and failure of the joint may occur as mechanical fracture of the substrate rather than cohesion failure of the sealant.

Substrates commonly encountered in the building envelope can be divided into broad categories as shown in Table 1.1. Guidance on the selection of sealants and primers for use with particular substrates and combinations of substrates is given in Section 2.3.4, and Table 2.3.

Table 1.1 *Common substrates by category*

Masonry	Architectural metals	Timber	Glass	Plastics
Granite	Copper	Treated wood	Monolithic	Acrylic
Marble	Bronze	Untreated wood	Laminated	Polycarbonate
Sandstone	Brass		Insulating	Fibreglass
Limestone	Steel		Reflective	Vinyl
Slate	Lead		Spandrel	PVC-U
Brick	Zinc			GFRP
Concrete	Mill finish aluminium			
Concrete block	Stainless steel			
Precast concrete	Vitreous metal			
	Anodised aluminium			
	Organic coated aluminium			
	Galvanised steel			

1.4.1 Masonry

There is a wide variety of masonry substrates, comprising porous and non-porous materials. Different sealant systems with different primers are appropriate to different masonry substrates, to ensure proper adhesion. If the joint designer is unfamiliar with a particular substrate, he should seek the advice of the sealant/primer supplier.

For rougher surfaces, care must be taken that the faces of a joint are smooth for the depth of the seal to ensure good adhesion. This can be achieved by the use of primers. Primers may also act as a barrier to migration from the sealant and prevent staining of natural stones.

Some very weak materials, such as lightweight concrete blocks and weak natural stones, may be over-stressed and crack as a result of high-tensile stresses imposed by the sealant in the joint. In this case, a low-modulus sealant should be used or a joint of different geometry (Section 2.8).

1.4.2 Architectural metals

Metal and coated metal surfaces have to be cleaned before sealing the joint. The use of low-tack tapes to protect surfaces on window and door frames may leave a residue of adhesive on the surface of the frame. Other contaminants will be present, depending on the method of handling and storage. Bare metal surfaces are tolerant of most degreasing agents, primers and sealants. Applied finishes to metal are not so tolerant of cleaning agents and sealing materials, and advice should be sought from the sealant and finishes manufacturers.

Some finishes to metal will separate from the metal before adhesion failure of the sealant occurs. For highly stressed joints it may be necessary to remove, or not apply, the finish on the area to be sealed. Note that sealing to mill finish aluminium can lead to corrosion of the aluminium behind the sealant and subsequent failure of the joint. Anodising of aluminium forms a non-separable coating that does not impair adhesion.

Coatings

Commonly architectural metals are coated to provide corrosion protection. Coatings fall broadly into two categories: those that provide active protection through electrochemical action and those that are inert barriers to the environment.

The former, generally zinc or aluminium, are applied by such processes as galvanising, anodising or direct metal spraying. In some cases, the porosity of the surface layer may then be reduced with a penetrating organic coating. Galvanised steel may be chromate-treated to prevent zinc corrosion during storage in damp conditions.

These processes should be considered as generic as, in each case, there are a number of basic modifications, together with numerous variables that may be controlled in a different manner. The nature and level of contaminants will also vary.

Although the corrosion resistance is seldom equal to that provided by an electrolytic process, some metals (e.g., aluminium) may be surface-treated chemically – primarily to control appearance and reflectivity.

These options can lead to many variations in the nature of the metallic surface (which may be further changed by relatively short weathering periods, i.e., months or less).

The consequent effect on sealant adhesion cannot be predicted with complete confidence. Discussion with the supplier, to determine whether testing is necessary, is therefore usually advisable.

Barrier coating systems, some of which may incorporate corrosion-inhibiting pigments, present a still wider range of surface characteristics. Most are based on organic polymers. They include the following broad categories:

- wet-applied air-curing systems, as dealt with comprehensively in BS5493, e.g., acrylics, vinyls, urethanes and epoxies, etc.
- stoved liquid paint and coatings applied as powders, e.g., polyesters, polyvinylidene fluoride (PVF2 or PVdF) epoxies and acrylic enamels, etc.
- thermoplastic coatings applied by dipping into a liquid (a plastisol) for example, PVC.

Proprietary coatings of a given type can vary significantly from one manufacturer to another. They normally incorporate a number of functional components, selected and optimised according to the preference of the individual supplier. The exact composition of a particular product may also be changed from time to time and without notice.

1.4.3 Timber

Timber is generally finished with paint or a micro-porous finish. The adhesion of these finishes to the wood is far inferior to that of finishes to metals and separation of the finish from the wood is a likely mode of failure.

Timber finishes that contain waxes, oils and silicones can cause adhesive failure of the sealant in the joint. Sealants have to be compatible with the finished timber product. Note that some timbers contain natural oils and waxes. For instance, teak and oak contain tannin, which may attack sealants and affect adhesion.

1.4.4 Glasses

Uncoated glass gives little cause for concern when using sealants. However, care may be needed with some coated finishes to glass. A greater problem is the use of sealants in contact with the edge seals of insulated glazing units. The sealants used in the edge seal of these units should be compatible with the other sealants to be used or curing may be inhibited.

Some glass is treated with an outer wetting coat to reduce the need for window cleaning. These coatings may seriously impair the adhesion of sealants.

1.4.5 Plastics

In general, plastics are easily damaged by solvents. Problems may arise from the use of solvents and other products to clean plastic surfaces. Solvent-borne sealants such as acrylics will also damage plastic surfaces.

Plastics may have surface coatings or residues such as mould releases that can cause adhesive failure in the sealant joint. Uncoated plastic surfaces may not provide sufficient adhesion either. A minimum solvent wipe may be necessary, but this should be tested before wide-scale use to check that it is effective and does not cause damage.

PVC-U is commonly used in the building envelope. PVC-U window and door frames are normally sealed to masonry and concrete using low-modulus silicone sealants.

Glass-fibre reinforced plastics (GFRP) are most commonly based upon thermosetting unsaturated polyesters fabricated by a moulding process. A first (external) layer of unreinforced resin (the 'gel coat') is used to give enhanced protection, appearance and weathering resistance. The exact composition of the surface coat may vary and should be checked for compatibility with cleaners, primers and sealants.

If there is doubt about the use of a particular sealant on any plastic substrate then either the supplier of the plastic component should be consulted or test specimens made.

1.4.6 Proprietary materials

Proprietary building panels and materials vary widely and include mineral boards, phenolic laminates, renders and so on. In general, the supplier of the panels or material should be consulted. Alternatively, test specimens can be made and tested. Consideration must be given to the long-term performance of the joint and issues such as discoloration.

1.5 COMPONENTS OF THE BUILDING ENVELOPE

Many of the principles of joint design are applicable to all parts of the building envelope. However, particular elements of the envelope give rise to specific problems. Sealing at the interface between two different forms of cladding often requires greater attention than the joining of similar components. The sealing of lightweight components is often more complex than the sealing of heavyweight cladding systems as the thermal movements are so much greater. The use of better insulation within the cavities of walls leads to greater thermal movement in all such cladding systems irrespective of material. Specific components of the building envelope are described below along with particular issues for designing joints within or around them. The detailed construction of sealant joints is covered in Section 4.

1.5.1 Concrete panels

Precast concrete may take the form of full-bay panels (panellised) or smaller units (unitised). Joints between panels or units have to accommodate all calculated movement as the panels or units are very stiff. Joints may be sealed with gaskets, wet-applied sealants or cellular sealing strips, or they may be left open. Windows may be sealed into rigid openings in large panels or sealed between smaller units.

Movement of smaller units depends on the method of fixing. Movements will be large if they are supported on the edges of floor slabs.

Tolerance for precast panels and units should be as good as for other factory-made components; they should be agreed with the manufacturer during panel and joint design.

1.5.2 Brickwork

Loadbearing brickwork behaves very differently from that supported on a structural frame. Movement joints in loadbearing brickwork are widely spaced and no horizontal joints are required. Non-loadbearing brickwork may be supported on a structural frame either as an external veneer or as a backing wall. Backing walls may be full-size infill

movements including floor deflections. Unitised curtain walling may be of heavyweight construction such as precast concrete units. However, it is often of lightweight construction, for instance GRP panels. With some lightweight panels, thermal and moisture movement may be the principal issue.

Tolerances for unitised curtain walling should be as good as those for window and door frames. In most cases, single components will span from top to bottom of a unit or a unit will be created in a single mould. Only for complex assemblies is there a case to accept larger tolerances.

1.5.9   Curtain walling (panellised)

Curtain walling may be factory-assembled in panels of storey height and of structural bay width (Figure 1.1). Built on structural steel strongbacks or as precast panels the sealing of the panels one to another may be by the use of sealants or gaskets. The location of joints is clearly defined and all movement must be accommodated at each floor line and each column line. However, the movement of the units is limited as they are fixed to the stiff elements of the primary structure on or near to the columns.

Panels may contain windows and doors and may comprise stone, metal or glass components. Sealing of the components within a panel will require the same considerations as for sealing them into any other wall. However, the panel may be more flexible than an in-situ construction and due allowance must be made for the movement of all the components that make up the panel.

Tolerances on panellised curtain walling, whether of steel or precast concrete construction, have to be agreed with the manufacturer at the time of panel and joint design.

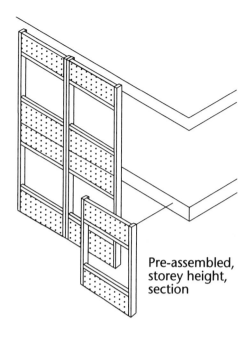

Unitised system

Pre-assembled, storey height, section

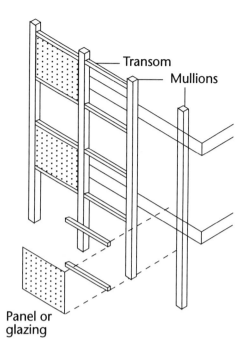

Transom

Mullions

Panel or glazing

Stick system

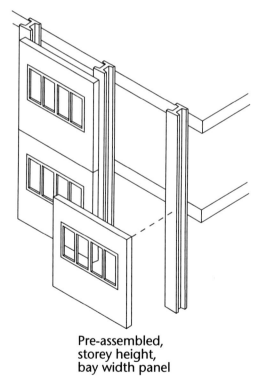

Pre-assembled, storey height, bay width panel

Panelised system

Insulation and cavity

Original structure

Support bracket

Over-cladding Panel

Rainscreen over-cladding

Figure 1.1 *Types of cladding*

1.5.10 Flashings and sills

Lightweight components such as flashings and sills may be fixed by an adhesive sealant. This both seals the joint and provides a hidden fixing for a component that is of aesthetic importance. If no mechanical fixings are present then the sealant joint must either accommodate the thermal movements or resist the resulting stresses.

1.5.11 Parapet cappings

The fixing of lightweight metal parapet cappings to a wall is complex, but consideration has to be given to the mechanical fixing of the joints between adjacent elements of the parapet capping. Problems of tearing of the sealed joints at low temperature are similar to those for metal roof panels. The joint between the parapet and the cladding below may be difficult to make with a wet sealant. In many cases it will be better to use an open joint appropriately lapped and ventilated.

1.5.12 Roof glazing

As with curtain walling, all glass-to-frame joints should be sealed with gaskets unless the roof is a structural silicone glazed system or an open-jointed 'patent glazing' system. Movement joints and joints to adjacent building components will be made with sealant or will be open joints that are lapped and ventilated.

Roof glazing systems are often supported on steel structures of medium to long span that are comparatively flexible. All joints should be designed to accommodate the consequential large thermal and structural movements.

1.6 BUILDING AND ENVELOPE MOVEMENTS AND THEIR CAUSES

For each structure and its cladding the major movements should be identified. They should each be described by magnitude and type and all considered in the design of joints. They include:

- thermal movement
- moisture movement
- floor loading
- wind loading
- snow loading
- vibration
- settlement and heave
- creep
- seismic sway

This section of the guide describes the causes of movement in the building and its envelope. It describes the nature of the movement, its likely magnitude and factors affecting its occurrence. Calculation of expected movement and joint width to accommodate this is covered in Section 3.3.

Movement caused at joints can be characterised as slow, intermediate or rapid and as tension, compression, shear or combined direct and shear movement. Section 3.3.1 gives further information on types of movement. Unloading, as well as loading, on a building makes demands on the sealant joints.

1.6.1   Thermal movement

Elements of the building envelope will undergo variations in temperature. During the day, radiation from the sun will raise surface temperatures well above the ambient air temperature. By night, radiation from the surface can reduce the temperature. The temperature change of a component is dependent on its orientation on the building, any localised shading of the component, its colour and surface finish (its emissivity), its thermal mass and its connection to the other building elements, particularly any insulation behind it. For rainscreens and other walls containing cavities near to their outer surface there is little conduction of heat to or from the building structure and the temperature swing is accentuated. Similarly, the recent move towards better-insulated buildings often leads to designs in which the cladding is insulated from the rest of the elements and has little thermal mass; again, the temperature range experienced by the cladding is accentuated. Typical service temperatures are given in Table 3.2.

Each facade of a building will experience a different temperature range depending on the building orientation and shading. In particular, north-facing facades in the UK will not experience extreme solar heating. It may be appropriate to use different joint designs on each facade.

Increases in the temperature of a component will cause it to expand, but if it is prevented from expanding either a compressive stress will develop in the component or it will buckle or ripple to relieve the expansion. Note that corrugated surfaces will resist rippling in the direction parallel to the corrugations while in the other direction movement will be absorbed with little visual effect.

Corrugated surfaces and other curved surfaces will allow shortening to take place in one direction. Where no mechanism to relieve contraction exists then the components will carry large tensile forces. A sealed joint between such components will tear apart unless adequate mechanical fixing of the component is provided.

Installation temperature

The amount of contraction or expansion that occurs at a joint will depend on the temperatures at which the components are installed, their size, the method of fixing and the temperature at which the joint is made. Component temperatures are the important criteria, not air temperatures. Component temperatures will differ widely from air temperatures. This is particularly the case for components heated by the sun. Sealant joints should not be made at component temperatures below 5°C; this limits the temperature rise that can occur after sealing. Sealant joints can be made between materials at elevated temperatures but care should be taken to set an upper temperature limit for installation if the design of a joint is critical and the material is designed to be fully extended in service (Section 5.3.1). Setting the upper component temperature limit for installation at 40°C will reduce the temperature fall that can occur after the joint is made and so limit the opening movement or force at the joint. Expansions and contractions are given in Table 1.2 for some typical components on the assumption that the sealant in the joints is applied with component temperatures in the range 5°C to 40°C in the UK. The method for calculating thermal movements is given in Section 3.3.2.

Curved panels

Curved panels when heated or cooled move normal to their surface. This arises because a uniform expansion or contraction leads to a change of radius. If the straight edges of the panel are restrained against movement a further movement occurs due to induced bending in the panel.

Thermal bowing

Surface temperature change can cause thermal bowing of elements. For components that are good conductors the temperature of the component will quickly become nearly uniform through its thickness and only expansion or contraction will take place. For components that are good insulators the inner surface of the component will experience a smaller temperature change than the outer surface. The different rate of expansion or contraction of the two faces leads to bowing of the component. This can be a particular problem for composite insulated panels and plastic infill panels. Note that for glazing frames, even thermally broken frames, the inner face of the component is likely to be warmed by incident radiation passing through the glazing.

Thermal bowing of components is not generally a consideration in the sealing of joints as it gives rise to an out-of-plane movement that is normally restrained at the panel edge. Sealing of panels edge to edge gives little problem, but sealing joints between dissimilar panels should take account of possible differential movement. Flashings and sills that are fastened with an adhesive sealant may bow and break loose if not adequately restrained.

Table 1.2 *Thermal movements of some common building components*
(assumes sealant application within the temperature range 5°C to 40°C for components)

Component	Dimension	Temperature of component		Max. fall (40°C - min °C) °C	Max. rise (Max °C -5°C) °C	Contraction	Extension
		Min °C	Max °C				
Aluminium glazing bar	1200 mm	-20	60	60	55	1.7mm	1.6mm
PVC-U glazing bar (white)	1200 mm	-25	60	65	55	5.5 mm	4.6 mm
PVC-U glazing bar (dark)	1200 mm	-25	80	65	75	5.5 mm	6.3 mm
Window opening (brick)	1200 mm x 1200 mm	-20	50	60	45	0.7 mm	0.5 mm
Aluminium mullion	3200 mm	-25	60	65	55	4.9 mm	4.2 mm
Steel panel (light)	1200 mm x 1200 mm	-25	60	65	55	0.9 mm	0.8 mm
Steel panel (dark)	1200 mm x 1200 mm	-25	80	65	75	0.9 mm	1.0 mm
Steel sheeting (dark)	6000 mm	-25	80	65	75	4.7 mm	5.4 mm
Steel sheeting (light)	6000 mm	-25	60	65	55	4.7 mm	4.0 mm
Aluminium sheeting (dark)	6000 mm	-25	60	65	55	7.0 mm	6.0 mm

1.6.2   Moisture movement

Elements of the building envelope and the building primary structure undergo movements as their moisture content changes. Durable impervious materials are not subject to moisture movement. Movements occur as one-off movements immediately following construction or as repeated movements. One-off movements occur as the water used in mortars, concrete and render dries out from the fabric and generally leads to shrinkage. Repeated movements occur as a result of seasonal, or more frequent changes in moisture content of the building fabric. Calculation of moisture movement is described in Section 3.3.3.

Initial moisture movement takes the form of component contraction, with the exception of clay or shale bricks, which may expand. Shrinkage of components in the building envelope will lead to an opening up of any sealant joints that are not fixed against movement. For fixed joints contraction of components will cause a tensile load in the joint and possibly shrinkage cracking of the component. Shrinkage of the primary structure will lead to a closing of the sealed joints in the building envelope. Typically the columns of a reinforced concrete frame may contract between 3 and 4 mm in each storey height and reduce the width of horizontal joints in the building envelope. Most of the initial movement occurs in the first six to 12 months of the building's life and should normally be assumed to occur after the joints have been sealed. Particular problems may arise where a brick panel expands within or over a concrete frame that is shrinking, and appropriate joint design is necessary. A rule of thumb is that all masonry panels on concrete frames should have a 15 mm expansion joint at each storey height. However, there is no theoretical basis for this figure. After initial movement, shrinkage proceeds more slowly and reversible movements due to moisture become more significant.

Expected moisture movements are of similar magnitude to thermal movements and joints should be designed to accommodate moisture movement of stone, brick and concrete elements. Particular attention has to be given to moisture movements in timber constructions and for timber elements of the building envelope; dimensional changes are particularly large in a direction across the grain.

1.6.3 Building movements due to loading

Building primary structures deflect under load and impose movement or loads on the building envelope (Section 3.3.4). The structural loads that cause movement are:

- floor loading
- wind sway
- snow loading
- seismic loading
- differential settlement and heave

Sealant joints should be capable of accommodating all movements that occur after the joint has been sealed. Movements that occur before the joint is sealed may affect the dimensions of the gap to be sealed. CIRIA Technical Note 107: 1981, *Design for movement in buildings*, gives guidance on the movements that may occur. However, the structural engineer should normally calculate anticipated building movements.

1.6.4 Floor loading

Floor deflections will give rise to building envelope movements only if the cladding or curtain walling is supported from the edge of the floor slab or a floor beam. Allowable deflections for structures of different materials are given in Table 3.5. Floor slabs may deflect up to 30 mm in some cases. Deflections in the range L/250 to L/500 are considered acceptable by the structural engineer, dependent on the type of cladding.

Part of the floor deflection will be due to the weight of the cladding and part to the occupation loads. If the resulting deflection of the building envelope is too great, consideration should be given to supporting the wall elements off a braced frame spanning between columns or stiffening the edge of the floor slab (Section 3.3.4).

If no provision is made to adjust the position of the wall components after fixing and before sealing of the joints, then the sealant joints will have to tolerate any movement that occurs during fixing due to the weight of the cladding.

Sealant joints should accommodate all movements occurring from loads applied after they have been sealed. These include dead loads from the construction of internal partitions as well as live loads on the floor. The differential deflection between consecutive floors is often more critical than the absolute deflection of one floor. Full consideration of the sequence of loading on each floor and the combinations of loading on two floors may lead to a more economic joint design.

1.6.5   Wind sway

Wind loading will cause structures to sway such that each floor experiences a different horizontal displacement. The joints in the building envelope should be capable of accommodating the differential floor movement that occurs at each storey. This movement should normally be accommodated within each storey height.

Sway of a building structure will lead to the movement of building envelope panels. The exact movement will depend on the nature of the cladding and its fixing. Wall and roof systems can accommodate movement by one of five mechanisms:

1. Individual panels distort over a storey height. This implies that individual panels are flexible in shear or can accommodate movement by rotation of a rigid panel within a flexible mounting, Figure 1.2(a). This may be a glazing rebate with gaskets.

2. Individual panels rotate and the vertical joints between them accommodate shear movement, Figure 1.2(b).

3. Individual panels rotate and both the vertical and horizontal joints between them accommodate shear movement, Figure 1.2(c). Note that care is needed in the detailing of the cruciforms of the joints.

4. Panels do not rotate but translate relative to each other. The horizontal sealed joints between the panels then have to accommodate shear movement, Figure 1.2(d).

5. Parts of the storey height are relatively rigid in shear and movement is accommodated in a more flexible band of the building envelope. This may be a band of ribbon glazing that is designed to accept movement of the glass units within their frames, Figure 1.2(e).

Building primary structures may experience very small sway movements if they are braced-bay frames or contain shearwalls. Unbraced frames will experience much larger sway movements.

Braced-bay concrete frames and structures containing masonry or concrete shearwalls transmit horizontal loads to the ground through large truss or plate structures. These stiff structures undergo displacements of up to 3 mm in each storey height. Buildings containing lift shafts will generally be of this form.

Moment-resisting frames of steel or concrete construction transmit horizontal loads to the ground by flexing of the columns, beams and floor slabs that are connected together by rigid moment-resisting joints. Movements are greater than those for stiffer structures, but sway movements are limited to 1/300 of the storey height in any one storey unless greater displacements can be justified having due regard to the type of cladding. The building envelope and its joints have to be designed to accommodate horizontal movements of 8 to 20 mm in each storey height. Note that industrial buildings may undergo considerably larger movements. Joint design may be simplified and more economic joints may be achieved if the joints, the cladding system and the fixings are designed at the same time.

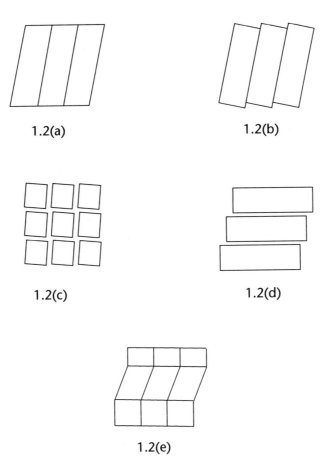

1.2(a)

1.2(b)

1.2(c)

1.2(d)

1.2(e)

Figure 1.2 *Accommodation of sway*

1.6.6   Snow loading

Snow loading will give rise to movements in roofing systems and these may be significant where a flexible support is used such as a steel portal. This may have implications for the sealing of penetrations through the roof. Snow loading may also give rise to movement at any joint where the roof interfaces with an adjacent wall or gable. If movements due to snow loading are believed to be significant the structural engineer should be consulted to ascertain what movement can occur.

1.6.7   Vibration

Components of the building envelope may vibrate as a result of traffic, plant, wind and pedestrians. With the exception of industrial buildings the extent of vibration in the building envelope should have been limited to create a comfortable habitable environment. Problems may, however, occur when secondary structures such as flagpoles or signs penetrate the building cladding. Such joints should be sealed with an elastic sealant and consideration should be given to using a conservative joint design.

1.6.8 Settlement and heave

In any structure the foundation of one part may settle more than that of another. For rigid structures of masonry, or those built on rigid foundations, settlement is unlikely to give rise to distress in cladding systems or sealant joints.

For framed structures of steel, concrete or timber the structural design codes allow for differential settlement of 1/500 of distance between adjacent columns. This value should be used in the absence of more detailed information from the structural engineer. The building envelope will then have to accommodate differential vertical movements of 10 to 20 mm in any one structural bay. Note that this is in addition to wind sway.

For some buildings designed to accommodate large differential settlements, such as mining subsidence, the building settlement movement may be greater than 1/500 of distance between columns. The advice of the structural engineer should be sought in these cases. It will often be necessary to design the joints, cladding and roofing panels and their fixings at the same time.

If a primary structure contains movement joints to accommodate differential settlement, the building envelope must have corresponding movement joints. These will have to accommodate concentrated localised movement of the envelope.

1.6.9 Creep

Long-term loading on the building may lead to creep in some members of the supporting structure or cladding. This problem is pronounced for timber structures, but it also affects concrete structures. Under a constant load a structure will first undergo elastic deformation. Creep will then allow the structure to deform further over a relatively long period of time although no further load is applied. If movements due to creep are likely to occur the structural engineer should be consulted to determine the likely movement.

1.6.10 Seismic sway

Earthquakes cause buildings to sway, creating building envelope movements of the same type as those due to wind loading. These movements are likely to be greater than wind sway movements and 1/200 of storey height is an often-used limit for differential horizontal floor movement.

It is necessary to establish with the structural engineer and client the movements to be accommodated by joints in the building envelope. It is acceptable for joints to lose their integrity at a lesser movement than that which causes the loss of structural integrity of the building envelope.

2   Materials used to seal joints

2.1   GENERAL DESCRIPTION

The following materials are used to seal joints on the external envelope of the building:

- gaskets
- sealing strips or tapes
- sealants

Rubber membranes that are bonded over the face of a joint, using a site-applied adhesive, are frequently used to effect a seal, e.g., on water-retaining structures, bunds and diaphragm walls. With the occasional exception of some remedial work, their use on the external envelope of buildings is uncommon as they would usually present an unacceptable appearance. However, they are used to form an air seal over concealed joints within some facades.

2.1.1   Gaskets

Gaskets are flexible materials, preformed and precured with various profiles, which must remain under compression to function effectively. They can be of solid or hollow section and may be formed from either cellular or non-cellular materials. They are based predominantly on rubber or a plastic (cork is an exception).

Gaskets represent a distinct approach to sealing joints and are not dealt with in this document. They are, however, discussed in detail elsewhere (CWCT: 1996, BPF: 1993, BS4255: 1986).

2.1.2   Sealing strips

Sealing strips (or tapes) are flexible materials, preformed in a range of sizes and sections, which also rely on compression, although some adhesion to a joint face may take place.

They may be considered as a special type of gasket and are of two basic types:

- mastic strips, usually manufactured from a relatively soft, tacky synthetic rubber to which an easily removed backing paper is applied
- cellular strips, usually based on a synthetic polymer, which may be impregnated (e.g., with a wax, rubber or bituminous compound) and may also be edge-coated with an adhesive layer (protected with a removable backing paper).

Mastic strips require initial compression to ensure proper adhesion to the joint components. A degree of compression must also be maintained in service. As these strips show little, if any, tendency to expand, they are unsuitable for joints that open beyond their assembled size.

Cellular strips may be supplied in a precompressed form to facilitate installation. They should be of a suitable size for the degree of compression specified by the supplier to be maintained throughout the range of joint movements anticipated.

Mastic strips are not considered here, but preformed cellular strips are discussed further in Section 2.2.

2.1.3 Sealant systems

Sealants are wet-applied materials formulated to both solidify (cure) in-situ and adhere to the joint surfaces in a controlled manner. The sealants considered in this document are cold-applied, non-cellular materials that are based on synthetic polymers.

Polymeric compositions that foam in-situ are widely available in a pre-packaged form, commonly a pressurised container (aerosol can). They provide a convenient means of filling gaps that occur within buildings. However, they are not classified as sealants within the present context and generally are unsuitable for use in movement joints.

Sealants must always be treated as a system, as additional products are essential for effective performance – back-up materials, bond breakers and (where recommended) primers or surface conditioners. Although these materials require only a relatively brief discussion, their importance cannot be emphasised too strongly as many premature failures are due to their misuse or omission (Sections 2.3.1, 2.3.2 and 2.3.3).

Joint fillers

Joint fillers, non-adhesive materials that are very compressible in comparison with the joint components, are used during construction to pack (and thus form) deep movement joints in brickwork, masonry and in-situ concrete. They are not generally used in building envelopes constructed from thin preformed components. They are briefly discussed below (Section 2.3.1) as they have several useful functions (Section 3.2.2).

2.1.4 Product ranges

The classification given above becomes increasingly complex as each type of seal is extended to show the range of generic materials used, the individual products that are commonly available and the variation in properties that can be obtained. This complexity has arisen for the reasons given below and is the main factor determining the need for this section of the guide:

- as the performance of the external envelope depends so critically upon the material used in any sealed joint, there is a continual search for improvement in reliability and durability, i.e., to design out sensitivity to workmanship, the application conditions and the service environment
- extensive resealing is invariably difficult and expensive and, consequently, product systems with a long effective service life are required
- the demands that have to be satisfied vary widely and cannot be met by a single material; a range of products is required to accommodate variations in the extent and rate of joint movement, the application and service conditions and the nature of the joint surfaces
- proliferation also occurs because polymeric materials are numerous and extremely versatile, giving the formulator or compounder many options for tailoring products to the needs of the user

- a competitive market, with frequent over-emphasis on the initial cost of products, also generates many alternatives.

The following discussion deals predominantly with high-performance, wet-applied sealants. Emphasis is placed on performance properties and information to aid selection. An understanding of the chemical nature of materials can also assist in their selection and use. Such background information, omitted here, can be obtained from the Bibliography.

2.2 PREFORMED CELLULAR SEALING STRIPS

2.2.1 Types

Preformed cellular sealing strips (tapes) are usually supplied in a precompressed (roll) form to facilitate installation and are manufactured from various synthetic polymers, such as PVC, polyethylene and polyurethanes. One side of the strip, which comes into contact with the substrate, is often coated with a self-adhesive layer, protected before installation by a thin release tape.

These strips are available with a closed cell structure (possibly surface-treated) or with an open cell structure that is homogeneously impregnated with an appropriate compound during manufacture. The nature and quantity of this impregnation is primarily responsible for the performance properties of the strip, e.g., movement accommodation, UV-resistance, durability and weathertightness. Rather than blocking the open cells, impregnation can convert them into a hydrophobic form. Consequently, these strips can provide weatherproof joints while still allowing moisture vapour to diffuse from the interior of the building envelope.

2.2.2 Installation

These strips, which are normally precompressed to between 15% and 20% of the original thickness, may be used in two ways:

- direct installation into a joint
- initial bonding to the joint face of one (pre-positioned) component.

The re-expansion rate depends upon the temperature of the strip, typically requiring one to two hours at 20°C. This allows sufficient time for insertion into existing joints, while the self-adhesive edge provides location until expansion is complete. When the strip is initially bonded to one component, the second component must then be compressed squarely to give the required joint width. In both cases, it is important that the strip is not stretched longitudinally during installation.

Ideally, the joint faces should be parallel. However, provided compression is maintained within the required range during service (Section 2.2.3), a certain degree of tapering may be tolerated. Beyond this point, it may be possible to accommodate a variable joint width by use of different strip sizes. This procedure should be discussed with the supplier as the simple butting of different strips may not be effective.

Although priming is often unnecessary (the supplier should be consulted), the substrates must be free of contamination and weak, friable surface layers. The surfaces should also be as smooth as possible – the tolerable irregularity should be checked with individual suppliers. These limitations apart, the strips are suitable for use with most substrates (staining should not occur) and they may be applied under conditions that are unsuitable for some wet-applied sealants, such as cold, wet conditions.

2.2.3   Properties

These strips are supplied in a wide range of sizes and it is essential that the correct dimensions are selected for given joints. The strips need to be maintained under a degree of compression throughout the range of joint movement in order to function effectively. The supplier will normally provide detailed advice on the strip size and the compression required. For watertight and weatherproof joints, a high degree of compression is necessary (typically down to between 20% and 30% of the original, i.e., uncompressed, width). However, for air seals in drained joints or for sound/thermal/ draught insulation, a lower level of compression is generally satisfactory.

The performance of the strip also depends upon an appropriate depth:width ratio. A value of 2:1 is normally required at installation, with 1:1 not being exceeded in service; i.e., the width of a movement joint should never exceed the seal depth.

Appropriate strips can accommodate high movement levels (MAF of 25% – Section 2.8) and durability in excess of 20 years is proven. However, it must be ensured that the specific type of strip has adequate exposure resistance for the proposed service conditions.

2.3   WET-APPLIED SEALANT SYSTEMS

As noted earlier, sealants should be treated as a system since various additional materials contribute significantly to effective performance. The typical joint details given in Figure 2.1 illustrate the use of fillers, back-up materials and bond breakers with sealants applied to appropriately primed surfaces. While it is beneficial to obtain all of these components from the same supplier, it is essential in the case of the sealant and the primer/surface conditioner to ensure compatibility.

These ancillary materials are discussed below (Sections 2.3.1–2.3.3), and a general introduction to the high-performance sealants mentioned in this report is given in Section 2.3.4. The performance properties of these sealants are considered in detail in Sections 2.4–2.10. Maintenance and resealing are discussed in Section 2.11, and Section 2.12 deals with the selection and specification of high-performance sealant systems.

2.3.1   Joint fillers

Function

In addition to their initial function during construction, joint fillers provide the following (often in combination with a bond breaker or back-up material):

- assistance in controlling the depth of sealant in the joint
- a firm backing, which forces the sealant against the opposing sides of the joint during application and tooling, thus assisting surface wetting and good adhesion
- a barrier to debris that could subsequently inhibit joint closure.

For joints that present two sides, such as some glass assemblies, it is necessary to apply a temporary backing, which is removed after cure of the sealant.

Types

Fibreboard and cork, supplied in sheets or strips and often impregnated with bitumen or other materials, and cellular plastics and rubbers are commonly used as joint fillers. Loose or braided mineral/synthetic fibres are also used on occasion and can provide improved fire resistance if needed (Sections 1.5.5 and 2.7.7).

The materials used to impregnate joint fillers may be extracted by solvents used to clean surfaces or those present in primers/surface conditioners. Consequently, care is required to prevent the spread of contamination that may be detrimental to appearance and sealant adhesion. Without separation by a bond breaker/back-up, discoloration of the cured sealant may also occur due to migration from the filler.

For several reasons, expanded polystyrene should not be used as a joint filler. It has insufficient resilience and can leave the sealant unsupported; additionally, its upper service temperature is relatively low, it is readily attacked by solvents in primers/surface conditioners, and its compatibility with sealants is very limited. However, more suitable cellular synthetic polymers are useful where load transfer across a joint must be strictly limited.

Properties

Joint fillers should be compressible and resilient, while being sufficiently stiff to act as a former for the joint during construction and resistant to extrusion from the joint, non-staining and resistant to handling and water-induced damage. With the exceptions noted immediately above, fillers generally do not have a direct and initial influence on the performance of the sealant itself. However, adequate compressibility is essential where unacceptable compressive loads could otherwise develop across a joint, for instance in clay brickwork where the joint width is reduced in service due to moisture-induced expansion. Here, the stiffer types of filler (hemp, fibreboard, cork and similar materials) must not be used in expansion joints; cellular polyethylene, polyurethanes or foam rubbers are more suitable due to their higher compressibility (in contraction joints, provided predominantly to accommodate shrinkage, most types of filler are generally acceptable).

The properties of joint fillers are described further in Section 3.2.2 and Table 3.1.

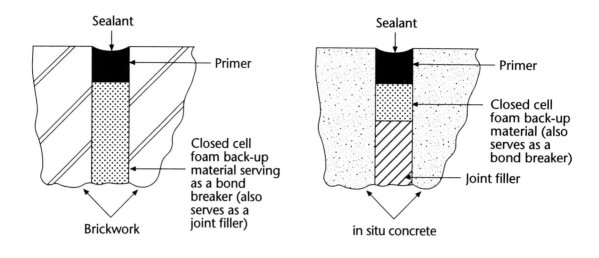

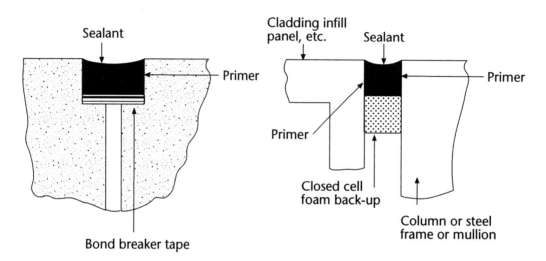

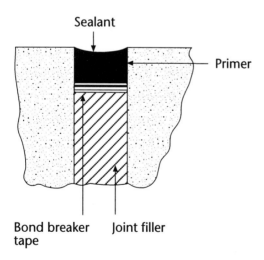

Figure 2.1 *Use of fillers, back-up materials, bond breakers and primers in sealed movement joints (from BS6093:1993)*

2.3.2   Bond breakers and back-up materials

Function

The use of bond breakers and back-up materials is illustrated earlier in Figure 2.1.

A bond breaker is a material applied to the back of a joint to prevent sealant adhesion to that part of the substrate or to the joint filler. Back-up materials are inserted in a joint both to control the depth and to define the rear profile of the applied sealant (Sections 2.8.2 and 2.8.3).

Back-up materials with appropriate surface release properties can also function as effective bond breakers, e.g., closed-cell polyethylene with a surface skin. Where this is not the case (e.g., polyurethane-based back-up materials with most sealants), a thin film bond breaker must be used for separation.

It is essential that the sealant is bonded only to the two opposing faces of a movement joint. Given two unrestrained surfaces, the mass of the sealant is then free to deform and to accommodate joint movements. Restraint, caused by lack of a bond breaker and consequent adhesion at a third surface, induces excessive localised stresses; premature failure of the type shown in Figure 2.2 is then likely to be observed.

Types

Self-adhesive strips of polyethylene or PTFE are commonly used as thin bond breakers as it is extremely difficult to establish an adhesive bond on these materials. Paper masking tape or PVC insulating tape can be used with some sealants; with many others, however, they become ineffective as a strong bond is developed. Relatively thin self-adhesive strips of polyethylene foam are also employed, particularly where a joint is too shallow for a thick section back-up material but too deep for a thin film bond breaker.

The preferred back-up materials are based on closed-cell cellular polymers, polyethylene, supplied in cut sections, sheet or rod form, being the most common. Closed-cell expanded rubbers (natural, EPDM or butyl) can also be used as back-up materials. Bond breaker tapes may then be required. Separation may also be necessary to prevent sealant discoloration due to the migration of antioxidants and extenders from the rubber.

Open-cell materials, e.g., polyurethanes, can absorb water by a wicking action, thereby maintaining potentially detrimental dampness behind the sealant. This problem is eliminated when the cells are closed, particularly in the case of polyethylene, which is inherently hydrophobic and is commonly supplied with a thin surface skin.

If the sealant penetrates the surface of a cut closed-cell back-up, an interlocking effect impedes separation, and hence the sealant's capacity to accommodate movement. Here, therefore, it is beneficial to use a material with small cells, particularly when the joint is designed to undergo substantial movement.

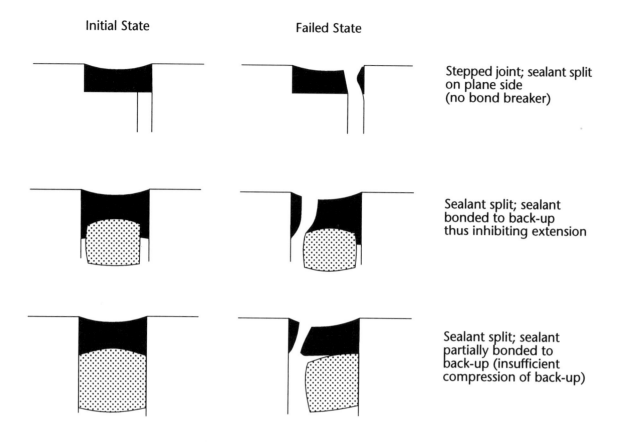

Initial State	Failed State	

Stepped joint; sealant split on plane side (no bond breaker)

Sealant split; sealant bonded to back-up thus inhibiting extension

Sealant split; sealant partially bonded to back-up (insufficient compression of back-up)

Figure 2.2 *Cohesive failures resulting from sealant restraint*
(from Resealing of Buildings – a Guide to Good Practice *by R Woolman and A Hutchinson, 1994)*

Installation

Careful installation of undamaged back-up materials is essential. When groups of cells are torn or ruptured, a closed-cell back-up can pump air or gas, particularly in joints undergoing large cyclic movements, e.g., those between well-insulated panels of aluminium or plastic. This can cause permanent blistering in uncured or partially cured sealants.

Cellular back-ups, at least 20 to 25% oversized, are compressed into the joint initially. They can then follow the range of joint movement while providing continuous support for the sealant – particularly important during the early cure period when the sealant can easily become distorted. Various types of back-up misplacement, resulting from careless installation and/or under-compressed or undersize materials, can lead to sealant failures, as illustrated in Figure 2.3 and as summarised below.

- due to its relatively large section, rod-form back-up requires a deep joint; if the joint is too shallow, the sealant section may be too thin and may, therefore, be prone to cohesive failure (Figure 2.3(a))
- for rectangular section back-up, the depth should be at least half the uncompressed width to prevent buckling during joint movement (Figure 2.3(b))

- insufficient compression of the back-up material can reduce the effectiveness of tooling and also lead to misalignment (Figure 2.3(c) and (d)).

Use of circular sections can prevent buckling and misalignment (although adequate compression must still be provided) and also ease insertion.

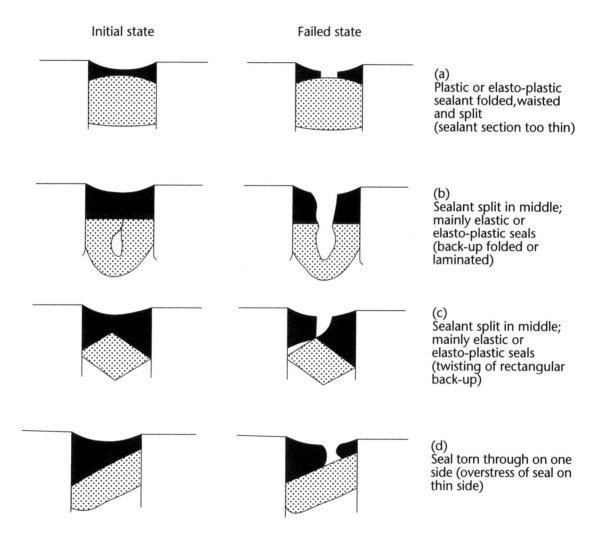

Initial state   Failed state

(a)
Plastic or elasto-plastic sealant folded, waisted and split
(sealant section too thin)

(b)
Sealant split in middle; mainly elastic or elasto-plastic seals
(back-up folded or laminated)

(c)
Sealant split in middle; mainly elastic or elasto-plastic seals
(twisting of rectangular back-up)

(d)
Seal torn through on one side (overstress of seal on thin side)

Figure 2.3 *Cohesive failures resulting from back-up misplacement*
(from Resealing of Buildings – a Guide to Good Practice *by R Woolman and A Hutchinson, 1994)*

Primers and surface conditioners

The need for surface preparation and priming

A major cause of the failure of sealant joints is inadequate preparation of the substrates, resulting in premature loss of adhesion between the sealant and the component surface. Good preparation involves three stages (Section 5):

1. **Assessment of the nature and condition of the surface.** The detailed actions required before sealant application can be defined and agreed on, a particular necessity where these are not itemised in a specification. Discussion with the sealant supplier may be advisable and, in some cases, testing may be required. Modern finishes especially can present seemingly similar surfaces that, in fact, vary widely in the characteristics essential for good adhesive bonding.

2. **Removal of contaminants such as dust, loose particles, corrosion products, release agents, oils and greases (including natural oils from hand contact).** Various types of abrasive treatment are commonly used. Cleaning with a solvent is often necessary. This should be performed only by experienced applicators and with advice from the supplier of the sealant and the component (solvents can be very aggressive towards many synthetic materials). All health and safety requirements must be complied with. For many sealant systems, moisture must also be regarded as a contaminant; natural or forced drying may be necessary. It is essential that precise definitions of dry, moist and wet are agreed, particularly for porous substrates.

3. **Application of the recommended primer or surface conditioner.** These materials improve the inherent adhesive strength and/or bond durability between a sealant and a well-prepared substrate. These are not recommended in all cases, but often they are omitted where they should be used, which inevitably is detrimental to performance. The specific product specified by the sealant supplier must be used, as formulations are matched to particular sealants and substrates – it must not be assumed that the commonly available variants are interchangeable. The need for a primer/surface conditioner can most obviously be appreciated where porous (e.g., concrete) or inert surfaces (e.g., plastics, synthetic finishes) are encountered.

Failures

The omission or incorrect use of primers/conditioners can result in the type of failures, mostly adhesive, illustrated in Figure 2.4.

Types and functions

There is no rigid or formally agreed distinction between primers and surface conditioners. However, conditioners may be defined as materials that chemically modify a surface at the molecular level, giving greater compatibility with the sealant, whereas primers are generally film-forming products.

Surface conditioners, also referred to as 'chemical primers', are dilute solutions of a reactive chemical, usually based on a silane and conventionally known as a coupling agent or adhesion promoter. The end-groups on the silane molecule differ, one having a strong affinity for the substrate and the other for the sealant. Ideally, a single molecular layer provides a strong and stable chemical link between the sealant and substrate. Similar adhesion promoters may also be incorporated in some primers and sealants.

Film-forming primers, usually based on resins or other polymers, may provide a strong physical bridge between the sealant and the surface, although many also react with the sealant to give a chemical link.

Primers have additional important functions as they can:

- be formulated to bond effectively to porous surfaces that are damp (protection against rain can then be particularly important as excess moisture may be detrimental, reducing the open time, Figure 2.6)
- contribute significantly to the maintenance of adhesion under prolonged damp/wet service conditions
- assist in overcoming adhesion problems presented by joints formed from dissimilar substrates (although the advice of the supplier should be obtained as it is seldom possible to use two different primers)
- prevent staining of substrates (due to migration of various species from the cured sealant or reaction prior to cure).

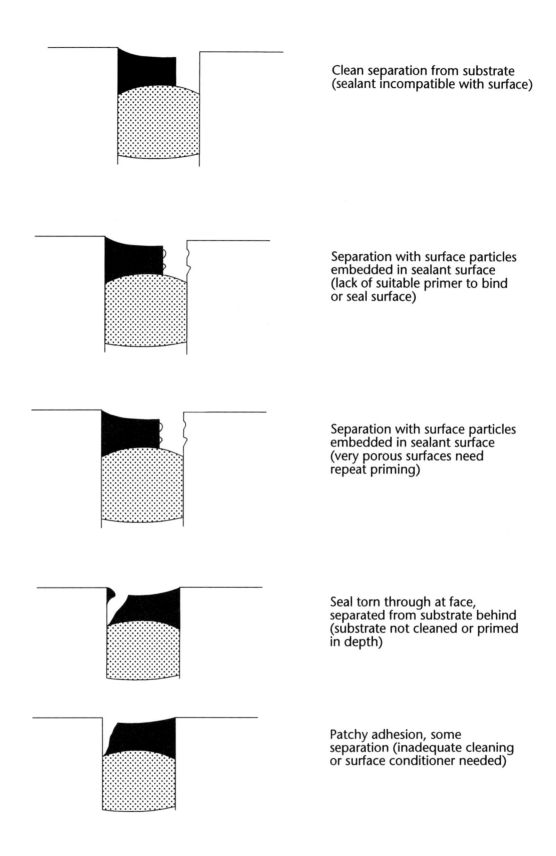

Clean separation from substrate
(sealant incompatible with surface)

Separation with surface particles
embedded in sealant surface
(lack of suitable primer to bind
or seal surface)

Separation with surface particles
embedded in sealant surface
(very porous surfaces need
repeat priming)

Seal torn through at face,
separated from substrate behind
(substrate not cleaned or primed
in depth)

Patchy adhesion, some
separation (inadequate cleaning
or surface conditioner needed)

Figure 2.4 *Adhesive failures resulting from poor surface preparation/priming
(from* Resealing of Buildings – a Guide to Good Practice *by R Woolman and A
Hutchinson, 1994)*

Porous surfaces

Primers for porous surfaces are usually designed for penetration, thus providing mechanical interlocking with the substrate, as shown in Figure 2.5. Due to their high viscosity, it is difficult for many sealants to wet thoroughly porous surfaces that are inherently very rough at a microscopic level. In addition to the more obvious concrete and masonry, primers may penetrate some metal alloy surface layers, e.g., anodised aluminium.

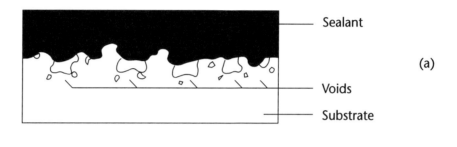

(a)

(a) Without primer

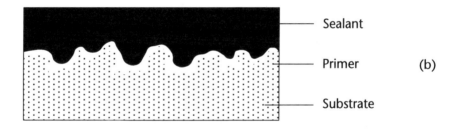

(b)

(b) Primer used to bind and consolidate surface

Figure 2.5 *Primers on a porous surface, showing also the principle of mechanical interlocking (from* Resealing of Buildings – a Guide to Good Practice *by R Woolman and A Hutchinson, 1994)*

Such primers can also assist adhesion by binding, and thus reinforcing, weak or friable surfaces and by reducing porosity (which can have a detrimental effect on the boundary layer of the sealant). Repeat priming may be necessary for very porous surfaces.

Open time

The interval between priming/conditioning and sealing may need to be controlled within certain limits, i.e., within the 'open time', as shown in Figure 2.6 and as recommended for the prevailing ambient conditions.

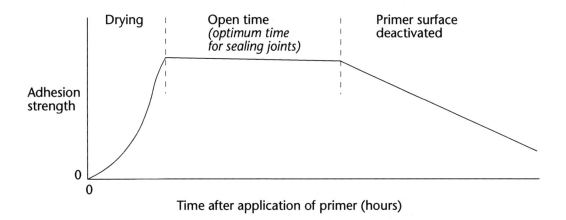

Figure 2.6 *Typical effect of open time of primers*
(from Resealing of Buildings – a Guide to Good *Practice by R Woolman and A Hutchinson, 1994)*

The lower limit is governed by the rate of solvent evaporation (in some cases, a primer component may interfere with the chemical cure of a sealant that is applied prematurely).

An upper limit is set if the primer becomes ineffective beyond this time – either because it dries to a hard film and the required tackiness is lost, or because the chemically reactive groups are neutralised by moisture or other constituents of the atmosphere. Careful programming of the work sequence is necessary when a primer becomes tack-free very rapidly, for example, in hot weather or on very hot substrates. If the recommended open time is exceeded, repriming is generally necessary; in some cases, the initially applied primer may have to be abraded or removed.

The applied primer must be protected against dust, rain and any other contamination.

Application

Primers must be carefully applied only to the joint surface, avoiding contamination of the external faces of the components. Most primers will affect surface appearance, some will stain and many will discolour and erode with exposure – appearance and weathering properties are not primary concerns in the formulation of primers.

It is normally recommended that the tape used to mask surfaces during sealant application should be placed before priming (Section 5.3.4). Primer should not be allowed to seep under the tape, causing staining and possibly bonding the tape firmly in place. Masking after priming may be preferable in some situations, for instance to prevent seepage on porous surfaces.

With primers that are designed to dry, back-up materials can be inserted easily after this stage has been reached. When the primer is soft and tacky, this operation becomes very difficult. If the back-up is installed earlier, care must be taken to prime the full joint depth, but not the surface of the foam where sealant adhesion must be prevented; the additional use of a thin film bond breaker may be necessary.

2.3.4   Sealants

Evolution

With the advent of curtain wall construction, particularly for high-rise structures, the external envelope of buildings became more flexible, both physically and in the scope offered to architects and designers (Section 1). The growing number of materials that can be used to prefabricate thin, lightweight facade components or to provide a surface finish has increased this scope still further. These changes have resulted in greater emphasis on the function of joints and generated a need for higher-performance sealing systems.

Traditional sealing materials – for example oil-based mastics or caulks – are generally relatively simple products, adequate for a range of ill-defined gap-filling operations where movement is minimal but usually possessing a relatively short service life (see below). Although these materials still have useful functions, newer products had to be tailored to more specific performance criteria as they had to provide:

- reliable adhesion to a wider variety of substrate types
- a capability to withstand a greater range, rate and frequency of movement
- improved durability in order to eliminate the need for regular maintenance on structures where access is often very difficult and there are considerable overall joint lengths.

Here, the formulator's task has been facilitated over the past 40 years or so by striking developments in the field of materials, synthetic organic polymers in particular. Consequently, a new class of product, the joint sealant, has evolved to supplement the more traditional mastics and caulks.

The terms high and low grade are occasionally applied to sealants. These can be misleading as 'low grade' could imply poor quality due to shortcomings in formulation/manufacture, thus rendering the material unsuitable for a given application. The description 'low performance' may avoid this connotation. Such materials can provide high quality in the sense that they perform quite satisfactorily the relatively undemanding function for which they are intended.

The justifiable projection of modern sealants as high-performance products should not obscure the fact that they do have limitations (although eventual deterioration does not necessarily imply faulty manufacture). As conveyed in Table 2.1, expectations should be realistic and it must be accepted that satisfactory performance will only be obtained if certain design and application requirements are implemented. The practical considerations listed in Table 2.1 are discussed in greater detail in the following parts of this section and in Sections 3 and 5.

Generic types

Table 2.2 provides a summary of generic sealant types and the main variations commonly used for movement joints on the external envelope of buildings. The particular joint types for which these sealants are generally suitable are summarised in Table 2.3. These summaries are provided as an introduction to the materials and to give an overview of their general characteristics and uses. The performance properties of these sealants and guidelines for their selection are discussed in greater detail in Sections 2.4–2.12.

Table 2.1 *Sealant systems: ideal versus reality*

Performance requirement	Practical consideration	Section
Accommodation of a wide range of movement (extent, rate and frequency)	Specific sealants are formulated to defined movement limits. To achieve this performance, joints must be correctly designed and sealant systems correctly installed. Misplaced emphasis on low initial costs can detract from performance.	2.8/2.7.4
Fewer sealant types, thus simplifying selection	Variations are generally essential to meet designer/user needs and a wide range of application/service conditions.	2.3.4
Any colour, a stable appearance and an absence of substrate staining	A wide selection of stable colours is available. Over-painting is often possible, but sealant performance may be affected.	2.7.6/2.8.3
	Staining can be avoided by use of the appropriate sealant and/or primer.	2.5.5/2.9.4
Good adhesion to any joint surface	Sealants and primers do not have unlimited tolerance. Substrates must be defined precisely, suppliers consulted and recommendations for preparation/priming/application must then be followed. One supplier must be used for the sealant and primer.	2.3.3/2.7.3/ 2.8.2
Good resistance to weathering and ageing	Performance may vary widely from one sealant to another. In-service materials and case histories should be evaluated. Specific additional testing may be advisable for certain projects.	2.9.1/2.10
No need for regular maintenance	On facades with a very long design life, any sealant is likely to require replacement at some point. All aspects of resealing should be allowed for at the design stage. Appropriate care over initial design and application should maximise the period to first maintenance. Initial cost-cutting may not be beneficial over the longer term, e.g., access costs will far outweigh material and labour costs.	2.10/2.11
Good storage stability	Recommended storage conditions must be used. Sealants that are beyond the stated shelf life must be discarded.	2.5.1
No need to mix	One-part sealants are readily available, but cure time can be slow; the effect of early movements may need to be considered.	2.5.2/2.5.4
Easy to mix	Two-part sealants must be thoroughly mixed in the correct proportion (pre-weighed, as usually supplied) using recommended equipment. Storage temperature may significantly affect the ease of mixing.	2.5.2
Easy to apply	Storage temperatures affect application characteristics. Joints should be designed for accessibility at the time of sealant application.	2.5.3
Tolerance to ambient conditions during application	Sensitivity varies; tolerance is not unlimited. Allowance for adverse conditions should be made in specifications. Cost savings achieved by initial misuse are likely to be insignificant compared to the cost of remedial work.	2.3.3/2.5.4/ 2.5.5/2.6.2/ 2.6.3
The lowest cost	Sealants represent a small proportion of the overall facade costs. Performance should take precedence over relatively minor savings in materials cost.	2.12

Table 2.2 *Some typical characteristics of wet-applied sealants*

Sealant type	Variation	Rate of cure	Accommodation of movement Amplitude *	Rate	Physical characteristic	Colour Range	Maintenance of appearance	Life expectancy (years)	Applicable British Standard
Acrylic	Solvent-based	Slow	Low-medium	Slow	Plasto-elastic/plastic	Wide	Average	15	-
Polysulfide	One-part	Slow-intermediate	Medium-high	Intermediate	Elasto-plastic	Wide	Good	20	BS5215
Polysulfide	Two-part, Low modulus	Intermediate-rapid	Medium-high	Intermediate-rapid	Elasto-plastic	Wide	Good	20	BS4254
Polyurethane	One-part	Intermediate	Medium-high	Intermediate-rapid	Elastic	Wide	Good	20	**
Polyurethane	Two-part	Rapid	Medium-high	Rapid	Elastic	Wide	Good	20	**
Silicone	One-part, Low modulus	Intermediate-rapid	High+	Rapid	Elastic	Wide	Excellent	25	BS5889

*   As defined in BS6093: 1993, Movement accommodation factors of 5% (low) 15% (medium) 25% (high) respectively. (Note: these represent total movement, not ± movement, Section 3.5.2.)
** Tested and specified according to other generic standards as appropriate.

Notes:

(i)   More rapidly curing grades of one-part polysulfides and polyurethanes are evolving.

(ii)   Gun grades are referred to: normal maximum width in vertical joints without slumping is 20 to 25 mm (some formulations to 30 to 40 mm).

(iii)   Appearance   Acrylics are subject to surface folds and dirt pick-up.

Polysulfides and polyurethanes often undergo surface crazing and chalking.

Silicones can exhibit noticeable dirt pick-up.

(iv)   Life expectancy is that anticipated under average exposure conditions.

62

Table 2.3   *Some typical applications of wet-applied sealants*

Joint type	Structural		Cladding					Perimeter sealing		
	Settlement	Expansion	Concrete, stone	Brick	Curtain wall aluminium	Metal panels	Plastic panels	Steel windows	Aluminium windows	Plastic windows
Movement type	Permanent distortion	Shrinkage Slow thermal movement	Slow cyclic	Thermal cyclic	Thermal cyclic	Thermal cyclic	Thermal cyclic	Thermal	Thermal	Thermal
Physical characteristic	Plastic Plasto-elastic	Elasto-plastic	Elasto-plastic	Elasto-plastic	Elasto-plastic Elastic	Elastic (Elasto-plastic)	Elastic	Plastic Elasto-plastic	Elasto-plastic Elastic	Elastic
Sealant type										
Acrylic	✓							✓		
Polysulfide (One-part)		✓	✓	✓	✓	(✓)		✓	✓	
Polysulfide (Two-part)		✓	✓	✓	✓	(✓)		✓	✓	
Polyurethane (One-part)					✓	✓	✓	✓	✓	✓
Polyurethane (Two-part)					✓	✓	✓		✓	✓
Silicone					✓	✓	✓		✓	✓

Notes:

(i)   All sealants are low-modulus grades.

(ii) More elastic sealants cannot necessarily be substituted for the more plastic types (and vice versa).

(iii) Applicable only to elasto-plastic sealants.

The following common sealant types are not shown in Tables 2.2 and 2.3 as they are not normally used to seal the movement joints discussed in this document:

- oil-based (oleo-resinous) mastics, mainly used for traditional glazing applications
- mastics based on butyl and similar synthetic rubbers, also used in glazing and to seal some lap joints between building panels
- bituminous compositions (including rubber or similarly modified products) used for joints in concrete pavements and water-retaining structures, etc.
- water-based acrylics, mainly used internally, e.g., perimeter pointing of doors/windows
- silicones designed for structural glazing
- high-modulus sealants designed for floors and other trafficked areas, e.g., flexible epoxy resins and some two-part polysulfides.

Fixed lap joints with a very low movement requirement are discussed elsewhere in this document (Section 4). Consequently, the characteristics of several low-performance mastics/sealants, not included in Tables 2.2 and 2.3, are given in Table 2.4.

Some of the sealant types given in Table 2.2 could be further subdivided to show other variations, for example, different cure mechanisms for silicones or different catalyst systems for polysulfides. However, this would exceed the intention of the summary and would not necessarily assist the designer, specifier or user. A suitable variation for a given joint should be reached by correctly and fully defining the application and service needs, initial reference to data sheets and discussion with suppliers.

The selection of proprietary products

The remaining task of selecting a specific proprietary sealant can be more difficult and requires detailed information; experience, familiarity with particular products, confidence in suppliers and specialist advice, etc., are also beneficial.

Different proprietary products of the same generic type can exhibit the properties generally required of a sealant to a varying degree. Consequently, to select a suitable product, specific requirements must be carefully and clearly defined. It may also be necessary to accept some compromise in balancing the requirements of individual cases (Section 2.12).

The final choice should not be varied by others to achieve small cost savings or to suit individual preferences. It should also be ensured that only the specified or agreed product is used. Attempts to justify substitution on the basis that the generic type is unchanged may well be over-simplified and could result in a completely unsuitable product being used. All sealants contain a number of components that are selected and optimised by the formulator. Hence, within a given sealant category, long-term performance can vary significantly as it depends upon this formulation detail. Random and unsupported substitution is unlikely to provide a better sealant than that initially selected on a rational basis.

Table 2.4   *Some typical characteristics of low-performance sealants/mastics*

Sealant/ mastic type	Accommodation of movement		Physical characteristic	Life expectancy (years)	Comment
	Amplitude*	Rate			
Oleo-resinous (oil-based)	Low	Slow	Plastic	Up to 10	Used for some perimeter pointing (not on PVC-U). Painting prolongs the effective life.
Bituminous	Low	Slow	Plastic	Up to 10	Used in roofing and where compatibility with other bituminous materials is required.
Rubber/bitumen	Medium	Slow	Plasto-elastic	Up to 10	As above.
Butyl	Low	Slow	Plastic	Up to 10	Used in concealed joints, as resistance to UV is poor. Wide variety of formulations.
Acrylic (emulsion)	Low-medium	Slow	Plasto-elastic	Up to 15	Used for internal joints/perimeter pointing.

* As defined in BS6093: 1993, Movement accommodation factors of 5% (low), 15% (medium), 25% (high) respectively

2.4   PERFORMANCE PROPERTIES OF WET-APPLIED SEALANT SYSTEMS

2.4.1   Cost-effectiveness

The prime aim in the selection of a joint sealant is to obtain satisfactory long-term performance at an acceptable cost. Economics prohibit use of the highest-performance sealant (with an implication of the highest cost) in all joints. A means of distinguishing products on a performance/cost basis is needed, preferably with an allowance for future resealing. This demands a methodology for the reliable and quantitative prediction of service life that can be implemented over short time periods. The number of resealing operations needed over the given design life of a building could then be estimated and costed. Although considerable research effort has been devoted to development of this methodology, it has yet to be defined precisely, for the following reasons:

- high-performance sealants are very complex materials that may be critically affected by many factors
- they are used in a wide range of environments with varying service demands
- the conditions and methods of application can determine length of service life
- longer and better-documented service experience is required to support the conclusions of laboratory work.

In the absence of an 'index' for cost-effectiveness, it is necessary to consider a number of initial properties, how these can change with time and how they may benefit or detract from the performance of a sealant. This can require some appreciation of the limitations of test data, for example, its dependence on curing/testing conditions that are standardised in the laboratory but highly variable on site.

Although the selection criteria may differ, lower-performance materials used for relatively undemanding applications, e.g., sealing of fixed low-movement joints, should also be cost-effective. Thus, although the accommodation of significant cyclic movement is not generally required, low cure shrinkage and an absence of staining potential do remain important.

2.4.2 National standards

Compliance with many national or other standards has limited implications and is seldom a completely adequate specification for the sealant. Such standards are valuable in providing agreed methods for determining certain characteristic properties (see below) and for monitoring production quality. In general, however, they do not provide assurance of in-service performance. Sealants complying with the same standard may also differ considerably, depending upon the exact details of the formulation and the specific applications envisaged by the manufacturer.

This position is changing, with potential benefit to the sealant user, as more comprehensive standards containing classes based on service requirements are evolving (Section 2.8.2). These standards will thus replace those that are currently based on generic sealant types, while standards providing improved test methods will continue to be developed.

2.4.3 Properties and testing

The important properties of high-performance sealants are considered in detail in Sections 2.5–2.9. These sections are presented in a sequence that follows the chronology of installation and service. Inevitably, therefore, certain key properties are discussed after others, which are usually less critical, at least in the design process. Where appropriate, properties are also considered in later sections – from the design aspect in Section 3 and with reference to application in Section 5.

Within the sequence adopted, movement accommodation factor and the shape of the sealant bead are dealt with in a separate Section (Section 2.8.1) in order to emphasise their importance (Section 3.5.2).

Several of the properties considered below are measured by standard test methods. Although the relevance of this information is discussed and comments on some procedures are given, testing details are generally taken to be beyond the required scope of this guide.

As background information on testing, the main content of a number of current standards is summarised in Table 2.5. Differences in the detail of test procedures are contained in the three British Standards applicable to generic sealant types (there are no equivalent British Standards for polyurethane or solvented acrylic sealants).

2.5 INSTALLATION PROPERTIES

2.5.1 Shelf life

The shelf life of a sealant is the period of time during which it remains unimpaired. This time period is always given on the container and data sheets. It is measured from the date of manufacture, so containers should be marked with an expiry date.

Sealants normally have a shelf life of six, nine or 12 months. The stated period is conditional upon containers being unopened and undamaged and upon proper storage (out of direct sunlight, protected from frost and in a cool (5 to 25°C) dry place). Puncturing of one-part sealant containers, in particular, will lead inevitably to a marked reduction in shelf life. An appropriate storage temperature will also ensure that the mixing, application and curing characteristics of fresh sealants are satisfactory.

Suppliers determine the shelf life using various test methods. However, all the properties specified should be obtained within the stated period provided the above stipulations are met. Once the expiry date is reached, sealants should be discarded. A usable consistency does not guarantee that other, less obvious, properties remain satisfactory.

2.5.2   Mixing and proportioning requirements

Sealants that are supplied as multi-part materials having two or more separate components must be mixed thoroughly in the correct proportion. This is essential for homogeneous cure, consistent properties throughout the mass of sealant and good colour matching from one pack to another.

The components of some grades are packed in layers in a single container and in the correct proportion. More commonly, the correct proportions are supplied in separate containers. It is essential that the entire contents are transferred into the mix, as a deficiency may affect the colour and the rate and degree of cure achieved. This can result in surface tack, a soft sticky mass or, at the other extreme, excessive stiffness.

Careful attention must be given to the mixing technique, following the supplier's recommendations and conventional good practice. A longer mixing time or excessive stirring speed will not automatically compensate for an inefficient mixing action and can be detrimental, causing heating and aeration (leading, respectively, to a reduced application time and a spongy cured sealant with reduced durability). Where components have a different colour, the loss of streakiness should not be taken as a guarantee of good mixing; a proven technique is to be preferred (Section 5.3.7).

Table 2.5 *Sealant testing – British and International Standards*

Standard	Main Title	Property
BS3712	Building and construction sealants	
Part 1 (1985)		Homogeneity, relative density, extrudability, penetration and slump
Part 2 (1973)		Seepage, staining, shrinkage, shelf life and paintability
Part 3 (1974)		Application time, change in consistency, skinning properties, tack-free time and adhesion of fresh material to mature sealant
Part 4 (1985)		Adhesion in peel, tensile extension and recovery and loss of mass after heat ageing
BS4254: 1983	Two-part polysulfide-based sealants	Rheological properties, plastic deformation (recovery), adhesion and tensile modulus, application life, adhesion in peel, loss of mass after heat ageing and staining
BS5215: 1986	One-part gun grade polysulfide-based sealants	Rheological properties, recovery and tensile modulus, adhesion and tensile modulus after heat ageing, cyclic adhesion and cohesion, adhesion in peel, loss of mass after heat ageing, staining
BS5889: 1989	One-part gun grade silicone-based sealants	Skin-forming time, resistance to flow (slump), extrusion rate, force on extension and elastic recovery, loss of mass after heat ageing, adhesion and cohesion in tension, staining, adhesion in peel
ISO7389: 1987	Building construction – jointing products	Elastic recovery
ISO7390: 1987	Building construction – jointing products	Resistance to flow
ISO8339: 1984	Building construction – jointing products – sealants	Tensile properties
ISO8340: 1984	Building construction – jointing products – sealants	Tensile properties at maintained extension
ISO9046: 1987	Building construction – jointing products – sealants	Adhesion/cohesion properties at constant temperatures
ISO9047: 1989	Building construction – jointing products – sealants	Adhesion/cohesion properties at variable temperatures
ISO10563: 1991	Building construction -sealants	Change of weight and volume
ISO10590: 1991	Building construction -sealants	Tensile properties at maintained extension after water immersion
ISO10591: 1991	Building construction -sealants	Tensile properties after water immersion
ISO11431: 1992	Building construction -sealants	Adhesion/cohesion properties after exposure to artificial light through glass
ISO11432: 1992	Building construction -sealants	Compression properties

Storage temperature

Storage at a low temperature, even within the range recommended for good shelf life, may contribute to poor mixing due to the higher viscosity of the components. However, unless the supplier gives specific instructions, temperatures above the recommended storage range should not be used to ease mixing.

2.5.3   Rheological properties

Pourable sealants are commonly available for sealing reasonably wide and upward-facing joints. Most sealants installed on the external envelope of buildings are gun-applied and have a smooth, paste-like consistency. The rheology of such materials is usually complex, but the formulator can control it to give:

- an adequate rate of extrusion and flow into the joint
- an absence of slumping or flow from the joint (particularly at higher application temperatures)
- ease of mixing multi-part sealants.

An optimum balance of these characteristics will be obtained if the sealant has been stored at a reasonable temperature (preferably overnight, as most sealants are poor conductors of heat). This requirement applies less to silicones than to other sealant types as they are relatively unaffected by quite large temperature variations.

To prevent slumping from very wide joints, filling may have to be carried out in stages, possibly separated by a short cure period. This technique should only be attempted by skilled and knowledgeable applicators, preferably in consultation with the supplier. Where possible, such problems should be avoided at the design stage.

The reconsideration of excessively narrow (and inaccessible) joints by the designer is even more important as, quite apart from other deficiencies, such joints can be impossible to seal, notwithstanding the sealant's rheology and the applicator's skill.

Effect on adhesion

Apart from its effect on ease of use, the rheology of a sealant can have a significant influence on adhesion. If the sealant is too viscous at the time of application, it will be difficult to ensure that good contact and wetting of the substrate surface is achieved – the rheology of the material will not assist this essential process and tooling will be less effective. Silicones have a significant benefit here, as their viscosity is relatively insensitive to temperature changes and most formulations provide good surface wetting.

2.5.4   Application life

All multi-part sealants have a limited application life after mixing and they must be fully installed within this time (which may also be referred to as the pot-life or usable/working life). The following factors affect the application life:

- high or low temperatures respectively shorten or extend the application life
- large masses of some sealants generate heat as they react, thus shortening the application life; heat may also be generated by excessive mixing speed
- inadvertent contamination by water can shorten the application life of some sealants.

The application life given on product data sheets may refer to only one temperature. If so, further information should be obtained from the supplier to determine what allowance should be made for existing site conditions (alternatively, the sealant can be stored overnight at the quoted temperature). In general, temperature has a more significant effect on the mixing of multi-part sealants than on the application life.

The cure of one-part sealants begins once the cartridge is opened. However, unlike two-component sealants, which cure uniformly throughout their mass, one-part products cure progressively inwards from the surface. This has two practical consequences:

- application can be interrupted if the cartridge is temporarily resealed (inadvisable for other than relatively brief periods)
- tooling must be completed without undue delay and before the surface skin is formed (two-part sealants must be tooled before their bulk consistency changes significantly)

2.5.5   Effects on (or of) adjacent materials

Effects on adjacent materials

Cleaning solvents and solvent-based primers or surface conditioners may attack and permanently mar the appearance of plastic/GFRP components and paint finishes, including polyester or other powder coatings. White spirit is much less aggressive than ketones, esters, aromatic hydrocarbons or chlorinated solvents.

Of the sealants considered in this guide, solvent-based acrylics are most likely to have similar effects; as a result of the softening action of the solvent, they may also become welded to the surface of some synthetic materials.

Polysulfides have contained a component that reacts with the lime in cementitious materials, producing a purple stain. However, since a test for this effect has been included in British Standards for more than 20 years, it should not occur with current products.

One common type of silicone evolves a mildly acidic material (usually acetic acid) as a normal by-product of the cure reaction. Even with a primer, such sealants are unsuitable for use with substrates that are attacked by acids, for example, concrete, cement mortar, limestone, marble and some metals. While this corrosive action will not necessarily be detrimental to appearance, it is likely to result in poor adhesion.

In addition to these more immediate effects, a slower process of substrate staining can also take place, as discussed in Section 2.9.

These adverse interactions involving polysulfides and silicones underline a more general point: substitution for properly selected and specified sealants should not take place at the purchasing or site-application stage on the simplistic basis that the generic type is unchanged. It is also recommended that the supplier is consulted when technical literature leaves any doubt concerning sealant/substrate compatibility as unexpected effects can occur.

Effects of bitumen products

Bitumen and pitch-based damp-proof membranes, water-proofing/protective coatings or mastics/relatively low-performance sealants should always be considered as a potential problem. Their presence in the vicinity of joints that are to be sealed with high-performance sealants is a frequent cause of staining, either of substrates and/or the sealant itself.

These products are readily softened and partially dissolved by solvents and other organic compounds; brown stains may thus be spread over areas adjacent to the joint, particularly when substrates are porous. The constituents of these products can also migrate into cured silicones, causing a yellow-brown discoloration that intensifies over a period of several weeks.

If these problems are anticipated at the design stage, they may be eliminated by appropriate isolation using bond-breaker tapes or backing strips. Site staff must be alert where a coating or dpm has been mistakenly extended beyond a specified area.

Effects on adhesion

Perhaps the most common deleterious effect of other materials on the sealant system is that of poor adhesion due to the nature of a substrate surface. This can result from contamination deposited during handling (including the transfer of natural oils from the hands) or other site operations (or resulting from failed sealants). It may also include surfaces that are markedly different to the bulk of a component due to some routine feature of the manufacturing process, for example, release agents, sealers on metal surfaces, laitance on cementitious materials and matting agents in coatings. For sealants used on cementitious surfaces, good resistance to alkaline conditions is, of course, essential.

Other effects of adjacent materials

More specific examples of the effect of adjacent materials on the sealant include the following:

- air, moisture and volatile materials absorbed from the sealant system can be rapidly forced out of timber warmed by the sun, causing blistering of slow-curing sealants; this is less likely if rapid-curing products are installed late in the day
- some sealants may become discoloured by the migration of constituents from synthetic rubbers used, for example, as spacers, isolating strips or gaskets
- excessive surface moisture can cause blistering of one-part polyurethanes as the evolution of carbon dioxide, a normal part of the cure process, occurs too rapidly
- water-proofing treatments applied to masonry before joint sealing can adversely affect the adhesion of sealants; typical examples include silanes, siloxanes and silicones. Microporous and other preservative timber treatments can have a similar effect
- provided they are used correctly, acid-based masonry cleaners do not normally impair fully cured sealants (although the colour of some sealants may be changed). However, if used prematurely, they may interfere with some cure reactions and full cure may not be achieved; with one-part polysulfides in particular, obnoxious odours may be generated over fairly long periods.

2.5.6   Health, safety and environmental concerns

Health and safety is generally compromised when the risks associated with the use of materials have not been properly identified and when appropriate controls to prevent or minimise these risks have not been implemented.

Fully detailed guidance on all matters connected with health and safety can be found in the publications prepared by the Health and Safety Executive.

Health and safety – the user and supplier

In recent years, the general requirements of the 1974 Health and Safety at Work Act have been strengthened by new Regulations. The responsibilities for controlling hazardous substances are now defined in more detail and are legally binding (on a 'deemed to know' basis). Both suppliers and users (employers and employees) are directly affected by this legislation, which is exemplified by the following Regulations:

- the Control of Substances Hazardous to Health Regulations (COSHH) 1988 and later amendments
- the Personal Protective Equipment at Work Regulations 1992
- the Chemicals (Hazard Information and Packaging) Regulations (CHIP2) 1994 and related legislation.

The use of sealant systems in an external environment could easily be viewed as an operation where little attention to health and safety is required, particularly as manufacturers ensure, so far as they are able, that the inherent hazards associated with their products are minimised. However, as further discussed in Section 5, attention is necessary as cleaning solvents, primers and sealants can contain materials that are flammable and hazardous via inhalation and skin/eye contact.

The CHIP2 regulations require manufacturers' safety data sheets to outline the type of precautions that must be taken by the user. It is essential, therefore, to consult current data sheets before starting work. As these sheets also contain a description of the hazards associated with a product, they can assist COSHH assessments. However, only the user can properly assess the risks, as these will vary from one project to another.

Health and safety – the designer

Due regard of the legislation referred to above is essential once it has been determined that a wet-applied sealant system will be used. However, the detailed implications of the Construction (Design and Management) Regulations (CDM) 1994 are still being defined. This legislation could have a significant effect on the use of sealants as it demands that all issues connected with health and safety are addressed from the outset of a project. Particular care is required in the selection of materials and construction processes as it must be ensured that structures are designed to avoid or to minimise risks to health and safety while they are being built, maintained or repaired. The possible impact of the CDM Regulations is discussed further in Section 3.1.5.

Health and safety – resealing

When failed joints are resealed, additional health risks can arise during the removal of the existing sealant, especially if preparation procedures generate dust. Some earlier formulations, for example, contained particularly hazardous materials such as asbestos and polychlorinated biphenyls (PCBs).

Environmental concerns

There is now worldwide, and increasingly significant, concern with the emission of chemicals into the environment, whether during manufacture, use, disposal or as a result of degradation in service. As with many products used in construction, the environmental impact of sealant systems may have to be considered more closely, particularly those containing or requiring the use of volatile organic materials. However, in comparison with solvented surface coatings, for example, the use of sealant systems generally causes a much lower level of atmospheric contamination.

At present, the most immediate effect of environmental concerns on sealant use is connected with the storage and disposal of used packaging and waste products, especially where these are hazardous.

More generally, the overall environmental impact of materials such as sealants is difficult to classify in the absence of standard assessment methods.

While no agreed method for appraising the environmental impact of materials currently exists, it is clear that:

- sealants are often derived from non-renewable resources
- solvents may be used for joint cleaning
- primers containing solvents may be used
- solvents may be evolved during cure
- sealants generally have a reduced life compared to adjacent building components; removal and replacement are expected during the life of the building
- sealants cannot be reused or recycled
- disposal of used sealants can be difficult (as shown by difficulties in disposal of the chlorinated paraffin type as used in the 1970s).

On this basis alone, sealants would be regarded as extremely 'non-green' materials.

This issue is discussed further in Section 3.1.7, where the position of the specifier/designer is also considered.

2.6   CURING PROPERTIES

2.6.1   Types of cure

The sealants considered in this document (Table 2.2) cure by three mechanisms, viz.:

- physical drying as solvent evaporates (one-part acrylics)
- chemical reaction initiated by the mixing of components (two-part polysulfides and polyurethanes); in general, volatile materials are not released
- chemical reaction induced by exposure to atmospheric moisture and oxygen (one-part polyurethanes, polysulfides and silicones); these reactions usually produce a volatile by-product (with silicones there is often a noticeable odour).

By appropriate formulation, the manufacturer can control the curing time in all three cases. However, the degree of control that can be exerted is greatest for the two-part sealants where variations between very wide limits can be achieved. For one-part sealants, it is not possible to reduce the cure time below a certain level due to the dependence on natural diffusion processes. Application conditions also have a significant effect on the rate of cure, as discussed below (Section 2.6.2).

Physically drying sealants inevitably undergo potentially detrimental shrinkage during cure. However, this shrinkage tends to be less significant with solvented acrylics in comparison with the water-based products that are primarily intended for less demanding internal applications.

2.6.2 Rate of cure

On site

The rate of sealant cure is significant for the designer/specifier as it determines the period during which the sealant is particularly vulnerable to dirt pick-up, accidental/deliberate mechanical damage and, possibly, joint movement and adverse weather.

Once properly mixed, two-part sealants cure uniformly throughout their mass at a rate governed by the formulation and temperature. This rate, which can be fairly rapid, is not affected by humidity or the sealant depth.

Solvent-based sealants generally cure more slowly as the substantially dry outer layers progressively increase in thickness towards the centre. Thus, a firm surface gives no indication of the overall state of cure. Any factor that inhibits solvent loss will extend the time for full cure, for example, low temperature, high humidity, impermeable substrates, deep sections, physical shielding.

Similar considerations apply to reactive one-part sealants, although, in this case, as the diffusion of atmospheric moisture into the sealant is required, cure may be retarded if the humidity is very low. In general, temperature has less effect on the cure rate of these sealants than on the types discussed above, and guide-line cure data is often given in terms of sealant depth per unit time. A stipulation regarding the maximum sealant depth may also be given, particularly for polysulfides and polyurethanes, which become much less permeable to moisture vapour than most silicones as cure progresses.

The cure times given on data sheets must be used for guidance only as site conditions can be very variable whereas standard and controlled environments are generally employed for laboratory measurements.

Environmental conditions

Suppliers generally provide information on the temperature and humidity limits required for a satisfactory rate of cure. In the UK, the relative humidity is generally above 50%, which is more than adequate for all moisture-curing sealants. However, much lower humidities may obviously be met in other locations.

Very rapid cure or skin formation at very high temperatures may cause difficulties with joint filling and proper tooling of the sealant, resulting in poor adhesion.

Low temperatures generally have a greater influence on the cure rate of two-part sealants than the moisture-curing types (some silicones, for example, will cure at -30°C). However, the humidity may be very low at such temperatures. At close to 0°C, good adhesion can be a more significant problem than adequate cure, as condensation, frost or ice may be present on the surface. This condition may be maintained long after the air temperature has risen, as surfaces can remain cold for a considerable period when overnight temperatures have been low.

Laboratory assessment

Research literature sometimes states that many sealants require a considerable period to reach full cure and that the definition of this state is unclear (depending upon the method of measurement). This should cause doubts about the data supplied by manufacturers, however. For the user, full cure can be defined simply as the attainment of the required service properties, whereas research often demands a more precise definition linked to the exact extent of chemical reaction.

One further consideration, which is important in laboratory work, may also be relevant to site if test specimens are prepared and placed in covered or partially ventilated containers: different sealants should be kept quite separate, as the volatile by-product of one formulation can interfere with the proper cure of another.

2.6.3 The effects of joint movement during cure

The post-installation properties of sealants, determined according to standard test procedures and given on data sheets, normally relate to full cure (see above). However, in contrast to testing, applied sealants do not remain in an undisturbed state under controlled and constant conditions until full cure is achieved. Ambient conditions vary and joints will open and close, particularly in response to diurnal changes, irrespective of the state of cure. Consequently, sealants are often subjected to cyclic movement when they are only partially cured and the service properties are far from being fully developed. Irreversible movement (Section 1.1.3) may also have to be tolerated.

The consequences, whether in regard to premature failure or, especially, long-term performance, are very difficult to predict. There may well be a dependence on the relative rates of attaining quite different properties. For example (and in an oversimplified manner): if modulus increases more rapidly than bond strength, there could be a tendency for the bond to be weakened by early joint opening; if these rates are reversed, the sealant itself is more likely to be affected.

Joint closure may be detrimental, leading to distortion that becomes permanent as cure progresses and to loss of the optimum sealant profile (Section 2.8). Uneven bulges (or hollows due to joint opening) may also be aesthetically unacceptable, contrasting adversely with adjacent smooth components.

The extent to which these interactions lead to loss of performance is probably not truly known. More simple factors certainly cause many failures, e.g., lack of a primer, etc. However, the potentially detrimental influence of early movement may usually be alleviated by a complex interplay of various properties.

Sealant type and design considerations

Increasing attention is being given to the effects of early movement, possibly reflecting the current prevalence of sealant/component combinations that are likely to increase the possibility of failure if subjected to early movement, viz.:

- one-part sealants, which are convenient to use, but which often cure relatively slowly (faster cure is achieved with some more recently developed products)
- thin, lightweight components, well insulated from the interior and constructed from materials with a relatively low thermal inertia but a high coefficient of

thermal expansion, e.g., aluminium and plastics. High levels of diurnal movement are, therefore, likely, particularly with dark colours. In contrast, diurnal changes for stone and concrete will generally represent a relatively modest fluctuation, imposed on the more marked seasonal variation in joint width.

Temperature changes can be allowed for when calculating the minimum joint width required for the fully cured sealant (Section 3.5.2). However, it is not possible to design similarly for any effect of early movement on a partially cured material. Consequently, where there is particular cause for concern, the specification of a more rapidly curing product should be considered in consultation with the supplier.

Early movement should therefore be considered when examining premature failure.

2.7 SERVICE PROPERTIES

2.7.1 The effects of temperature

High temperatures

Temperature has a major influence on the performance of cured sealants as, generally, it is primarily responsible for inducing joint movement. However, for UK conditions, the maximum temperatures experienced by a sealant on a facade (approximately 80°C) are unlikely to have any directly adverse effects in the short term. Some sealants will soften more than others (the more elastic are the least affected), but this behaviour should not detract from the performance of a well-formulated product.

Over longer time-spans (10 to 25 years), high temperature is a critical factor in determining the service life. It will accelerate chemical degradation initiated by moisture and sunlight and thus contribute to the deterioration of physical properties, including adhesion. In more extreme climates, this degradation may be so rapid (five to 10 years) that it is better described as premature failure – this is most likely to occur where the humidity is very high or where the joint design favours moisture retention.

Low temperatures

Low (and falling) temperatures induce tensile stresses as joints increase in width. They can be particularly detrimental to the performance of sealants, therefore, if they also cause undue stiffness. The sealant itself may be unable to accommodate the imposed amplitude or rate of movement and fail cohesively. Alternatively, the higher stress generated at the sealant/substrate interface may lead to adhesive failure.

Two effects of decreasing temperature need to be distinguished:

1. An abrupt increase in modulus (by several orders of magnitude) at a fairly well defined and characteristic temperature (the glass transition temperature).

2. The more gradual and lower degree of stiffening which may occur above this transition.

In the first case, the molecular motion required for elasticity is effectively frozen and the material is transformed from a rubber to a glass. This phenomenon is frequently demonstrated by shattering rubber tubing with a hammer blow after it has been frozen in liquid nitrogen.

For the very elastic sealants, such as silicones, this transition occurs at such a low temperature that it is rarely, if ever, of concern, even in the harshest of climates. It generally takes place at higher temperatures for more plastic materials. However, for high-performance sealants, the transition will remain beyond the lowest anticipated UK service temperature. Consequently, these sealants should retain their essential visco-elastic character under winter conditions.

They will, nevertheless, be subject to the second effect noted above and will behave as stiffer materials with a reduced stress relaxation at lower temperatures. Depending upon the particular sealant type and formulation, there may, therefore, be an increased tendency for the type of failures noted above to occur. This stiffening can be particularly significant for the more plastic one-part acrylic sealants; at the other extreme, silicones and other elastic sealants are relatively unaffected.

The recommended movement accommodation factor (Section 2.8) should include an allowance for the possibly greater demands placed on the sealant by low-temperature strain (whether this is the case for specific products should be checked with the supplier). Where appreciable rates of joint movement are anticipated, an elastic sealant should be favoured, as the more plastic types may be unable to respond adequately at low temperatures.

2.7.2 Tensile properties

Modulus: isolated and bonded specimens

The modulus of sealants is a (possibly *the*) most critical service property, as it determines the tensile stress placed upon the sealant/substrate bond as a joint opens – particularly when stress relaxation cannot occur due to the inherent nature of the sealant (Section 2.7.4) or rapid joint movement. However, although data sheets routinely classify sealants as high- or-low modulus products, a value for the modulus may be omitted. This is because the evaluation of tensile performance using bonded test specimens (Figure 2.7) is ultimately more informative than the conventional determination of modulus using isolated sealant samples. The latter measurements are often used in research and development work where changes in the sealant are being investigated, but they are not used directly in design (Sections 2.8 and 3).

By subjecting bonded specimens to tensile strain, the effect of modulus on the integrity of the bond can be determined; ideally, ultimate failure should occur cohesively in the sealant, indicating that performance in service should not be compromised by inadequate adhesion. (Note: this description over-simplifies the testing that leads to suppliers' recommendations.)

The effective modulus

An effective or apparent modulus is often calculated from the results of the above procedure. This always represents a secant (or single point) modulus of the sealant in the bonded assembly (generally quite different to the Young's (tangential) modulus of the isolated material). Usually, this value is related to a specific extension, for example, the 25% or 100% modulus. The latter is directly equal to the induced stress at 100% extension, i.e., at unit strain. Where a constant cross-sectional area has been used in a series of tests, the secant modulus is occasionally given as a force (potentially confusing as 'modulus' then appears to have the incorrect units, i.e., N in place of N/mm^2).

The specimens shown in Figure 2.7 can be used to investigate variations of application and service conditions. Changes in secant modulus, stress and extension at failure and the mode of failure then indicate whether the performance of a sealant/substrate combination is significantly and adversely affected.

(Note: With these specimens, ultimate failure may be influenced by end effects. From one aspect, the specimens have an optimum depth/width ratio; from another, they represent a very short length of excessive depth, see Section 2.8.2.)

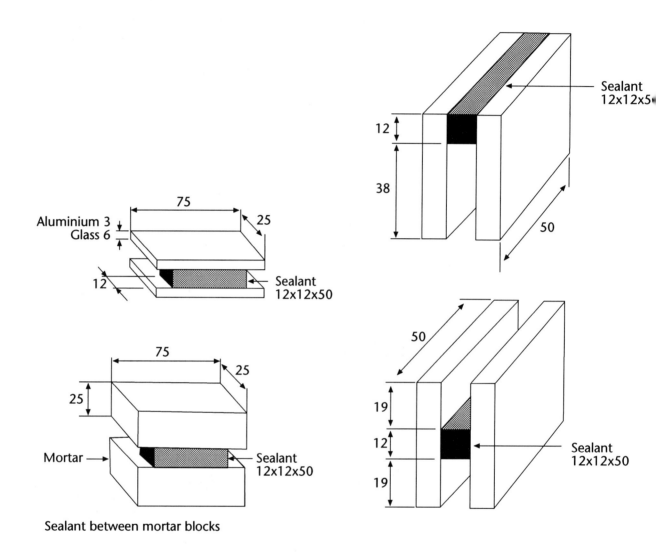

Sealant between mortar blocks

Figure 2.7 *Typical standard test specimens (all dimensions are in millimetres) (from BS5889:1989)*

Ultimate elongation and strength

One tensile property, the ultimate elongation, is often given on data sheets for sealants, although it might be better omitted. It has no value in design and is potentially confusing and misleading.

Many sealants will undergo an elongation of at least 500% before failure when tested in isolation from a substrate. However, recommendations for joint design normally limit movement to significantly lower levels (by at least an order of magnitude. Several factors contribute to this apparent discrepancy:

- in the absence of any other effects, service recommendations normally utilise only a proportion of ultimate performance
- sealants are not subjected to simple extension – they undergo repeated cycles of complex movement over long periods
- restraint by the substrate during extension can generate high stress concentrations – at the interface and both within the sealant and at its surface. Consequently, adhesive or substrate/sealant cohesive failure may be initiated at a far lower extension than the ultimate value given by the isolated sealant.

For similar reasons, it is also unnecessary to quote the ultimate tensile strength of a sealant. However, if a well-bonded sealant is subjected to a level of movement beyond that recommended by the supplier, or if the joint is too narrow (Sections 2.8 and 3.5.2) then failure in a tensile mode may occur, as illustrated in Figure 2.8.

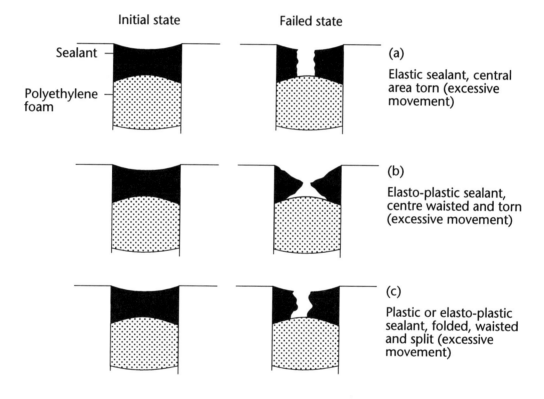

Figure 2.8 *Cohesive failures resulting from excessive movement*
(from Resealing of Buildings – a Guide to Good Practice *by R Woolman and A Hutchinson, 1994)*

2.7.3   Adhesion

The attainment and maintenance of good adhesion is essential for a sealed joint to remain weathertight. The successful performance of many joint lengths suggests that this aim can be fulfilled routinely and with relative ease. However, loss of adhesion is also the major cause of failure. Thus, while the achievement of satisfactory adhesion does not impose any particularly unusual demands, it does require close attention to detail at all stages, from design to installation. There is one additional key factor that should be kept in mind with all aspects of adhesion: high standards are not necessarily required for good initial adhesion but they are paramount for long-term performance.

Requirements

The basis of good adhesion can be stated very simply – intimate contact between adhesively compatible materials and the absence of weak or contaminated surface layers; the contributory factors are more involved.

It must be ensured, during design and construction, that excessive stress is not placed upon the sealant/substrate bond due to an inadequate joint width; joints must also be accessible, both in width and location – sealants are not designed to fill excessively small and remote gaps. Sealant systems must then be selected that are appropriate for the substrate, and surface preparation and priming needs must be clearly defined (Section 2.3). Inadequate adhesion can easily originate during installation when the following factors are critical (Section 5):

- surface condition – removal of contamination, acceptable moisture level
- priming – proper application of the correct type, observation of the recommended drying time
- correct placement of the back-up/bond breaker – to give the correct bonded area and to avoid three-sided adhesion
- the initial temperature of the sealant – particularly for products that become very thick when cold, as adequate contact and wetting of the substrate will then be difficult to achieve
- effective tooling – to remove air voids, to ensure good contact with the substrate and to obtain the correct sealant profile.

It is essential that close attention is given to these requirements throughout the sealing operation; poor adhesion, even on very few and scattered short lengths of a joint, can represent a major problem.

Adhesive performance can be influenced by the very earliest design decisions, as lap joints place less demand on the sealant system than butt joints, while fillet joints are the least desirable (Section 3.2.1).

Particular care over all factors affecting adhesion is most essential when very elastic sealants (e.g., silicones) are specified. These sealants exhibit relatively little stress relaxation compared to the more plastic products (Section 2.7.4) and tensile stresses are maintained at the bonded interface whenever the joint opens.

Different substrates

As discussed earlier, tensile testing of sealant/substrate specimens is fundamental to the evaluation of wet-applied sealing systems. The results of this work enable the supplier to give recommendations regarding generally suitable substrates on product data sheets. Very often, more detailed information will be available for specifically defined surfaces; consequently, consultation is always advisable. However, the increasing range of materials, particularly surface finishes, that are encountered in construction of the building envelope places greater demands on both sealant systems and suppliers (Section 1). Unfortunately, the provision of receptive surfaces is not a critical item in the manufacture of many components and changes in this process, not apparent to the end-user, can have a major influence on the adhesion of a sealant system.

Good long-term adhesion depends upon subtle and complex interactions at the interface, and generalisations with regard to generic surface types are inadvisable. Although non-porous surfaces can be characterised relatively easily and rapidly in the laboratory (methods may eventually become available for routine site-use), generally it is necessary to support these measurements with more time-consuming bond tests. It is essential, therefore, that suppliers are consulted at the earliest possible opportunity whenever there is a lack of proven performance with a particular substrate. It may also have to be accepted that recommendations are confined to initial performance as long-term adhesion can be difficult to assess and, therefore, to guarantee.

This emphasis on the importance of surface detail could appear to be misplaced as the adhesion tests given in many national/international standards utilise a substrate that is relatively uncommon in practice – sand/cement mortar. However, this approach does enable well-defined test pieces to be produced conveniently (by direct casting) and consistently, and experience has shown that test results can be extrapolated reliably to precast/cast in-situ concrete, irrespective of the specific mix design.

It may be desirable to use test pieces sawn from concrete in some circumstances, particularly when long-term adhesion is being assessed, for example, to determine the effect of an admixture or specific aggregate or to investigate the influence of different surface preparation techniques.

With regard to the latter, the universal recommendation that laitance must be removed from concrete surfaces is known to be frequently ignored or cursorily followed by superficial wire-brushing. Unpublished evidence suggests that laitance might be tolerated provided an appropriate penetrating primer is used. Concrete rather than mortar test pieces would allow the influence of laitance on adhesion to be investigated both more realistically and in detail. In this manner, research would usefully address actual site practice rather than the disregarded ideal.

Site assessment

For a variety of reasons, it can be desirable to assess the adhesion achieved under site conditions. Merely pressing the cured sealant, or applying stress by pulling a short section that has been cut free of the joint, may well reveal markedly poor adhesion (Section 5.4). A more controlled and quantitative method would be extremely useful, but at present there is no recognised test available.

Sealant-sealant adhesion

On occasion, even during new construction, good adhesion to a cured sealant must be obtained, for example, in branched joints, where destructive testing has been carried out or where sealant replacement is necessary. Depending upon the degree of cure, this can be difficult to achieve with some sealants (e.g., silicones and some polyurethanes) and the advice of the supplier should always be sought.

2.7.4   Visco-elasticity and dynamic response

Synthetic polymers and, therefore, the sealants considered in this document are visco-elastic, i.e., they are not perfectly elastic bodies. They exhibit what may be described as a delayed or damped elasticity. This is often represented by a combined spring and dashpot, where the latter (a loose-fitting piston in a cylinder containing a liquid) retards the response to an applied stress. One simple combination is shown in Figure 2.9.

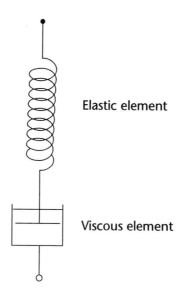

Elastic element

Viscous element

Figure 2.9 *Spring and dashpot representation of visco-elasticity*

This model assists in illustrating a qualitative classification that is conventionally applied to sealants:

- elastic sealants (most typically the silicones): the viscous (dashpot) element plays a relatively minor role and the sealant behaves much like a spring, responding immediately to an applied stress/strain
- plastic sealants (most typically the oil-, butyl- and bitumen-based products, which are not discussed in any detail in this guide): the viscous element plays a major role and the final (total) response to stress/strain is very delayed
- elasto-plastic and plasto-elastic sealants (typically, polysulfides, some polyurethanes, one-part acrylics and some silicones): both elements are significant but one or the other predominates to a degree, depending on which term is used.

The time-dependent response, or delay between cause and total effect, has the following consequences, which are important to the performance of sealants:

1. Creep, where there is a partially delayed strain response to a change in applied stress.

2. Stress-relaxation, where decay in stress occurs after strain is changed.

3. On removal of an applied stress, the rate and extent of recovery from deformation can vary widely (measurements of this type are most commonly used to classify the dynamic performance of sealants).

4. The material does not react in a simple manner to the imposition of cyclic movement as stress and strain become out of phase (an effect that will not be discussed further).

5. The relationship between stress and strain (and hence the modulus) is markedly dependent upon strain rate with obvious implications for both testing and service.

The effects of stress relaxation are illustrated in Figure 2.10 and strain rate in Figure 2.11.

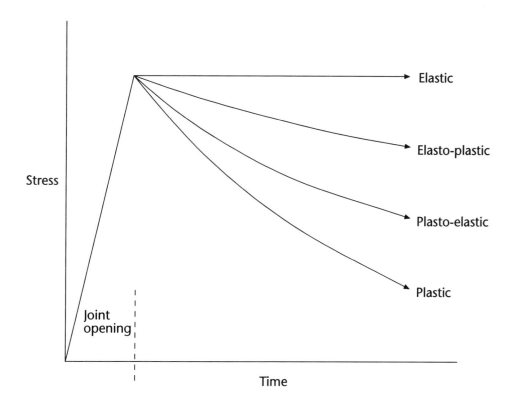

Figure 2.10   *Stress relaxation after joint opening*

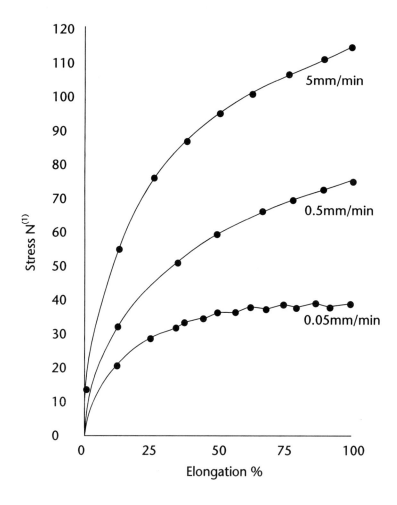

Figure 2.11   *Stress-elongation at different rates of strain for a typical two-part polysulfide sealant (from* European Adhesives and Sealants, *Vol. 3(1), 1984)*
(l) see Section 2.7.2 for explanation of units

When these effects are combined with the classification given above, the behaviour of sealants can be summarised as follows:

Elastic sealants

- the sealant responds immediately to joint movement and the induced stress is closely proportional to the imposed strain
- rapid recovery from deformation is observed when stress is removed
- the sealant is able to respond satisfactorily in joints that open and close very rapidly, e.g., those between thin metal or plastic components
- as there is relatively little relaxation, the stress imposed at the sealant/substrate interface is maintained; good adhesion and adequate joint width is, therefore, critically important (Sections 2.7.3, 2.8 and 3) and substrates must have a relatively high cohesive strength
- in general, these sealants are relatively unaffected by low service temperatures

Plastic sealants

- minimal (and slow) recovery from deformation occurs when stress is removed
- these sealants are only suited to joints where there is negligible and relatively slow movement; rapid movement is likely to cause cohesive failure, particularly if the sealant depth is inadequate (Section 2.8.2)
- creep may lead to bulging or necking with time when there is excessive slow movement
- at low service temperatures these materials may become appreciably stiffer

Elasto-plastic/plasto-elastic sealants

- these sealants can normally accommodate higher levels of movement than the plastic materials
- they are suited to slow-moving joints such as those formed from thick components/materials with a high thermal inertia
- stress relaxation assists in reducing interfacial stresses; although the design and installation demands are no less than for the elastic sealants, substrates with a lower cohesive strength may be better accommodated
- compared to elasto-plastic sealants, plasto-elastic types are uncommon.

Compression set

An effect related to creep (other mechanisms also operate) is commonly known as compression (or permanent) set. Part of the strain induced by a compressive stress becomes 'locked-in' and cannot be recovered even when the joint opens slowly. This phenomenon, in effect, reduces the usable width of the sealant, much as though the design width was too narrow. The more plastic sealants (e.g., one-part acrylics) tend to show a larger compression set than the predominantly elastic types (e.g., silicones).

This effect should normally be allowed for in the supplier's recommendations and special consideration by the designer is only likely to be required in exceptional circumstances.

2.7.5   Abrasion and tear resistance

Abrasion

Although abrasion resistance is an important property for sealants used in joints on floors and other trafficked surfaces or where there is severe water scouring. It is only rarely of significance on UK facades. The sealants considered in this guide should have quite adequate resistance to the mechanical action of wind-driven rain or solid particles (in desert areas, very strong winds and sand may cause marked erosion, particularly if the sealant is prone to surface chalking induced by sunlight).

Tear

Tear resistance may need to be considered because mechanical damage, whether accidental or by vandalism, may in principle initiate cohesive failure when the sealant is under tension – much as rubber splits fairly easily if it is cut while being stretched.

The more elastic sealants, such as the silicones, are generally considered to have the poorest tear resistance (a feature that is not assisted by stress retention during extension). This is probably more true of earlier formulations, but even here the tear characteristics did not cause major problems. Silicones can now be formulated specifically to eliminate the tendency for tears and similar damage to initiate further significant splitting as the joint opens.

Vandalism

Even with the most favourable properties, sealants with high movement accommodation can be seriously vandalised with relatively little effort. Harder, tougher sealants with much greater resistance to such damage are available, but the modulus of such products is generally too high for substantial movement to be accommodated. Consequently, on occasion, consideration may have to be given to other options, for example: recessing joints, adding cover plates or decorative trim, or providing a secondary sacrificial seal.

2.7.6   Over-painting

Mastics/putties

The low movement accommodation capability of non-setting mastics and putties relies upon the retention of a soft pliable mass protected by an outer skin of dry material. With ageing, the unprotected skin thickens and toughens, thus reducing the volume of pliable material and the ability to deform. Consequently, the over-painting of these materials is essential in order to retard the hardening process, which leads to splitting.

Sealants

High-performance sealants used in movement joints do not need to be painted to prolong service life and the protection described above is not required. Attempting to provide a barrier to more general weathering is unlikely to give significant long-term benefits. In some instances, painting may even reduce the service life of the sealant; when a paint film is less flexible than the sealant it is likely to crack and thus concentrate or localise surface strains, which can initiate premature cohesive failure.

Over-painting is generally undesirable, but in applications where adjacent substrates have to be painted after the installation of a sealant, either for protection or aesthetic reasons, it may be inconvenient or difficult to mask the sealant (particularly with fillet joints). A product that can be painted is then beneficial. Most acrylics, polysulfides and polyurethanes are inherently paintable (although the latter may inhibit the drying of some paints). Apart from special formulations, silicones cannot be painted successfully, as good adhesion to the cured sealant cannot be obtained.

Discussion with the sealant supplier is advisable when over-painting is being considered, both with regard to the type of paint and the timing of its application. Painting too early can inhibit cure of the sealant, by retarding either the loss of volatile components or the ingress of moisture vapour. The sealant may also be damaged permanently by the solvents present in the paint.

Colour

The majority of high-performance sealants are readily available in a reasonably wide range of colours. Consequently, there should be no need to paint new sealants simply to change the colour if this matter has been considered properly before specification, possibly assisted by appropriate mock-ups.

2.7.7   Fire resistance

The performance of materials, including sealants, under fire conditions is an area requiring specialist advice. Many standard test methods are available (for example BS476), but the results of these, or other specifically designed procedures, have to be interpreted in the context of applicable regulations and the particular combination of materials used on a given project.

Various fire-rated sealants are available that offer resistance via intumescent or ablative mechanisms. The use of these, or other sealants, needs to be considered as part of the overall design of a building, particularly as sealed joints on a facade are likely to be viewed very differently to internal joints (which may have to function as fire-stops).

Where there is a concern with fire breaking out from an external joint, mineral wool or ceramic fibres can be used as backing materials in place of polyethylene foam. A degree of fire-resistance is then conferred upon the joint, irrespective of the sealant type (Sections 2.3.1 and 1.5.5).

2.8   MOVEMENT ACCOMMODATION FACTOR AND SEALANT GEOMETRY

This section is concerned with various means by which the primary or inherent properties of a cured sealant (e.g., modulus and visco-elasticity) are converted into factors that can be controlled at the design stage.

While there is some overlap with Section 3.5, the following discussion provides a background to the design process, which is dealt with in detail in the later section.

2.8.1   Movement accommodation factor and sealant width

Design requirement

The key attribute of any sealant system is its continued ability to accommodate the joint movement imposed by the structure without any distress likely to lead to premature failure of adhesion or cohesion. With regard to the amplitude of movement, in tension, compression or shear, the capabilities are dependent upon material characteristics that are more simply conveyed by a composite property, the movement accommodation factor (MAF). Modulus, for example, affects the value of this factor (which is recommended by the supplier). However, it can be defined solely in dimensional terms that include a factor of safety, with obvious benefit to the designer/user.

The basis of the MAF: joint width and induced stress

The magnitude of this property dictates the minimum designed joint width that must be used if the strain (and hence the stress) induced within the joint is to be kept at an acceptable level. This can be illustrated by the following simple equation, which shows that stress is inversely proportional to the joint width (note: this equation is not used directly to derive or define the MAF):

$$\text{Stress} = \frac{\text{modulus} \times \text{change in width}}{\text{original width}}$$

Thus, for a given joint movement and sealant (modulus) the induced stress will be excessively high if the original width is excessively low (the basic reason why small cracks resulting from the omission of movement joints usually cannot be sealed effectively). Similarly, for given dimensional factors, high stresses will be generated by high-modulus sealants.

If this equation is rearranged, then it can be seen that, for a given sealant (and, therefore, modulus), <u>acceptable stresses</u> can be expressed simply in dimensional terms:

$$\text{Acceptable stress} \quad = \quad \frac{\text{change in width}}{\text{original width}}$$

This provides a basic description of the MAF, but the following points must be noted:

- the acceptable stresses are set by the supplier and take into account both adhesive and cohesive properties
- these stresses are not determined via a simple tensile test; a much more complex test regime is required so that service factors can be allowed for, e.g., different temperatures and substrates, cyclic movement, the effects of more extended periods under tension and compression and the influence of moisture, etc.
- considerable efforts have been made to develop test regimes that will yield realistic MAFs. However, it is extremely difficult to reproduce very complex service conditions in the laboratory
- test procedures have varied both with time and between one country and another. Through international standards, methods are becoming more uniform; however, significantly different MAFs for apparently similar sealants may still be found in trade literature. It is essential that such conflict is resolved by consultation with the individual suppliers
- the formal definition of the MAF has also varied because both the 'change in width' (M) and the 'original width' (W) have been expressed in different forms; i.e., M can be equated to tension (+) and compression (-), giving a ± expression, or more simply to the total expected movement, W can be equated to a mean joint width or to the minimum joint width.

Definition

The definition of MAF currently recommended in the UK (BS6093: 1993 and BS6213: 1982) is as follows (a butt joint is assumed):

$$\text{MAF (\%)} \quad = \quad \frac{\text{Total acceptable movement (mm)} \times 100}{\text{Minimum joint width (mm)}}$$

In this definition, therefore, the MAF is related to the full range of expected movement (M) between maximum compression and tension; the joint width (W) is a theoretical figure, or first approximation.

If W is initially determined from the MAF and M, allowances can then be introduced to allow for inherent and induced deviations, as described in Section 3. In this manner, a minimum designed joint width is obtained that incorporates a factor of safety (by taking account of the range of widths that could be met in practice).

It should be noted that, irrespective of movement accommodation, a width of at least 5 mm is essential for adequate access and reliable installation of the sealant.

Range

MAF values are described in BS6093: 1993 as being low (5%) medium (15%) or high (25%), with the rider that a figure of 50% is applicable to some sealants. In the past, an MAF of 100% (usually expressed as ±50%) has been claimed for many silicones. In general, such claims have been revised downwards with experience and with the introduction of more demanding test regimes. The BS6093 description given above has been used in Table 2.2 (note: higher modulus/lower MAF silicones and two-part polysulfides are commonly available for different applications to those dealt with in this document).

Lap joints

A lap (or shear) joint places far less stress on the sealant than the equivalent butt joint (for a given movement). Under appropriate conditions, therefore, a sealant will be able to accommodate greater movement in this configuration (Section 3.2.1). However, lap joints are usually more difficult to design into a structure and they are less easily sealed and maintained than butt joints (although they are more protected from weathering).

2.8.2 Sealant classification

A comprehensive system for classifying sealants used in glazing and construction is introduced in ISO11600: 1993, where detailed requirements and test methods for different classes are also stipulated.

This is essentially a performance standard where different generic types of sealant are not considered explicitly. Sealants are distinguished by use and classes of movement capability, viz.: glazing sealants (two classes) and construction sealants (four classes). Sub-classifications based on modulus (high/low) and elastic recovery (elastic or plastic sealants) are also included.

Further requirements for sealants in each category must also be met – many of the ISO test methods noted in Table 2.5 are used for assessment.

Unfortunately, ISO11600 uses a ± notation for movement capability while not clarifying whether this refers specifically to a test procedure or to an (undefined) MAF. Additionally, the standard does not fully address the relationship between classified sealants and suitable applications. However, the formal acknowledgement that movement capability, rather than generic type, should form the basis of a rational classification has considerable merit (while re-introducing an approach that was used in a deleted BS Draft for Development, DD69, 1980). Furthermore, ISO11600 is also supported by associated standards which have a logical basis, dealing with: terminology; application properties; and properties related to service performance (Table 2.5).

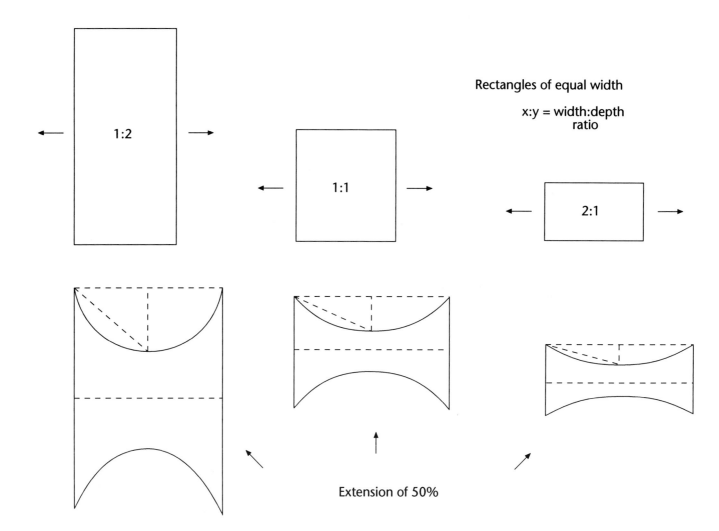

Rectangles of equal width

x:y = width:depth
ratio

1:2

1:1

2:1

Extension of 50%

Strain at surface > strain at central plane

Additional strain minimized by reducing depth of rectangle

Figure 2.12   *Effect of sealant depth on surface strain*

2.8.3   Sealant depth

When a sealant is extended, its volume is unchanged and a reduction in cross-section, therefore, has to take place. Restraint at the interface with the substrate prevents a uniform reduction and, consequently, a maximum loss in section thickness is observed at the centre. As illustrated in Figure 2.12, this generates a surface strain that increases with the original sealant depth.

Finite element analysis has also shown that these effects produce large stress concentrations at the boundaries of the sealant/substrate interface, as shown in Figure 2.13 below.

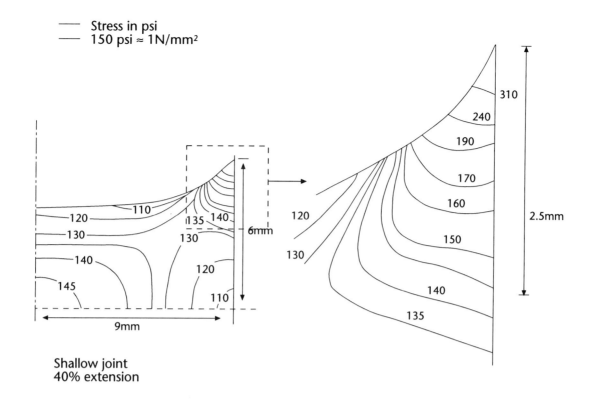

Shallow joint
40% extension

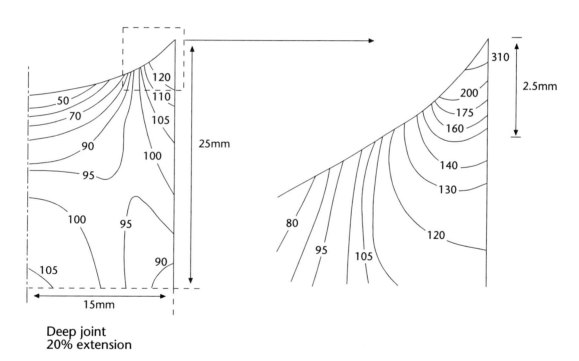

Deep joint
20% extension

Figure 2.13 *Effect of sealant depth on stress concentrations*
(from Adhesive Age, *March 1970)*

In the case of elastic sealants, these surface strains and stress concentrations need to be minimised, particularly in rapidly moving joints, as little stress relaxation occurs (Section 2.9.2). Consequently, the sealant depth is generally limited by stipulating that the width:depth ratio should be at least 2:1 (for more practical reasons and notwithstanding the above limitations, a minimum installed depth is also generally recommended).

For more plastic sealants, stresses are relieved by relaxation effects and deeper sections ensure the cohesive integrity of the sealant during (slow) joint movement. The following width:depth ratios are normally recommended:

- elastic sealants   2:1
- elasto-plastic sealants   2:1 to 1:1
- plasto-elastic sealants   1:1 to 1:2
- plastic sealants   1:1 to 1:3

Where sealants (or mastics) are employed as an adhesive filler, in essentially fixed joints, much deeper sections may be used (width:depth ratios less than 1:3).

For one-part sealants, an additional recommendation regarding the maximum depth is frequently made so that full cure is not unduly delayed.

2.8.4   Sealant profile

As shown in Figure 2.14, surface strains and stress concentrations can also be reduced by control of the sealant's profile (use of circular back-ups and tooling – Section 5.3.8). The design depth then refers to the centre of the curved face where the sealant depth is least. This requirement is generally more important for elastic, as compared to plastic, sealants.

Additionally, and for a given strain, a concave profile will result in a lower average stress over the bonded area.

2.9   LONG-TERM PERFORMANCE

2.9.1   Natural deterioration

Prediction

It is now generally accepted that the principal factors responsible for long-term deterioration of sealants – weathering and movement – operate synergistically. Consequently, there is a need for predictive test methods that utilise exposure regimes combining both influences. Currently, all-embracing procedures for evaluating service life are not available due to the difficulties posed by this task.

Weathering parameters, such as heat, sunlight and moisture, can be reproduced in the laboratory, but it is always difficult to apply this capability to predict service life. Over-acceleration has to be avoided, as it can cause anomalous degradation. Correlation between artificial and natural weathering is required and an appropriate balance of individual parameters has to be selected (i.e., the climate that is being reproduced).

Cyclic movement can also be imposed upon bonded sealant test specimens. However, reality is very complex and its simulation is complicated by factors such as a lack of detailed knowledge concerning joint movement and its effects and, also, the visco-elastic nature of sealants (which dictates that strain history is more important than in the case of many other materials).

Combining these approaches to provide a test method for quantifying service life is therefore difficult on a theoretical basis, leaving aside the more practical complexities and the need to assess a very wide range of substrates.

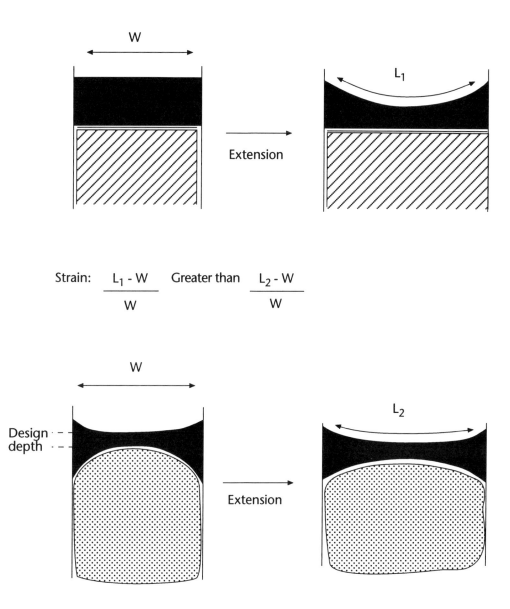

Strain: $\dfrac{L_1 - W}{W}$ Greater than $\dfrac{L_2 - W}{W}$

Figure 2.14   *Effect of sealant profile on surface strain*

A somewhat simplified approach could be of use to the designer, i.e., the determination of movement accommodation factors (using current methods) after extended periods of artificial weathering representing different climates. Bonded specimens both with and without an applied stress could be exposed. While the movement/weathering synergy would be omitted, the relative long-term performance (and appearance) of different systems could be usefully compared; the use of an 'after-weathering MAF' might then provide an added 'safety factor' at the initial design stage. This approach might also assist in directing joint design and sealant selection towards the more exposed elevations (e.g., south-facing) where deterioration is most likely to commence.

Types of deterioration

In the absence of more revealing test procedures, familiarity with the types of long-term deterioration that occur in practice can be very useful when durability is being considered during design and specification. The possible locations of long-term deterioration and failure are summarised in Figure 2.15 and discussed further below.

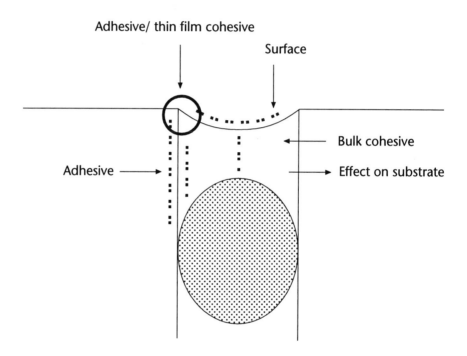

Figure 2.15   *Possible locations of failure*

2.9.2   Adhesive and cohesive failure

Adhesive failure

Long-term adhesive failure is most likely to be observed with elastic sealants such as the silicones and some polyurethanes/polysulfides, particularly if the modulus increases with ageing (more likely with the latter types). As a relatively low level of relaxation is obtained with these sealants, tensile stresses are maintained at the interface whenever the joint is wider than its initial dimension. Age-hardening will tend to increase the magnitude of these stresses, particularly at low temperatures (with some products). Depending upon the substrate type, particularly wet environments may also accelerate adhesive failure as, apart from stress, water is generally the most significant factor affecting adhesion.

Apart from underlining the need for suitable priming and good surface preparation, an eventual adhesive failure mode emphasises the importance of providing an adequate joint width initially in order to minimise interfacial tensile stresses.

Cohesive failure

Sealant failures that begin at the corners of the bead are often seen during testing and in service; failure propagates through the sealant, leaving a thin film attached to the substrate. This can be mistaken for adhesive failure, whereas it is a form of cohesive failure initiated by high stress concentrations at the extremities of the sealant/substrate interface. The more elastic sealants tend to be prone to this type of failure, particularly if the modulus increases during service. In addition to correct design of the initial joint width, proper control of the sealant shape and the width:depth ratio will assist in alleviating thin-film cohesive failure during service. A rectangular profile and an excessively deep section will favour high stress concentrations.

In testing, failure in a thin-film cohesive mode is acceptable, provided that the ultimate stress and elongation attain a satisfactory level.

With the more plastic sealants, the following effects can contribute towards thin film cohesive failure:

- loss of stress relaxation properties and an increase in modulus with ageing
- compression set (Section 2.7.4), which, in effect, may be equated to a reduction in the functional width of the sealant
- joint movements which are too rapid for stress relaxation to be effective.

The first two factors depend on the properties of the sealant. However, the designer can take account of the third by ensuring that joints that are likely to open and close at an appreciable rate are sealed with a sufficiently elastic sealant.

Unless the properties of an elastic sealant change markedly with time (or it suffers mechanical damage) bulk cohesive failures are most likely to be observed with the more plastic sealants; rapid or excessive joint movements and an inadequate width:depth ratio can encourage this type of failure.

2.9.3   Surface appearance

At the design/specification stage, likely changes in the surface appearance of a sealant can usually be considered only from knowledge of the general tendencies shown by different generic types. This may be supplemented by earlier experience with specific products or by examining in-service materials.

Sealants may undergo loss/change of colour, excessive dirt pick-up, embrittlement and crazing (which may induce cohesive tears and splits), wrinkling, chalking erosion and mould growth. These unsightly effects, mostly due to weathering action, depend primarily on the generic type, although the sealant formulation also has an influence.

Generally, the one-part acrylics and silicones have good resistance to weathering and their surface appearance is relatively stable, although the cured silicones are particularly prone to attract dust. The acrylics may also exhibit significant dirt pick-up.

Erosion (chalking) and consequent colour fading occurs most predominantly with polysulfides and polyurethanes and is likely to be most noticeable with intense colours, e.g., black/red rather than white/grey. Sealants of this type are also susceptible to surface crazing although (particularly with the polysulfides) the cracks usually remain quite shallow and do not propagate into tears or splits.

2.9.4   Staining of adjacent substrates

The migration of oil extenders/plasticisers into or onto adjacent surfaces is widely experienced with low-performance oil- and butyl-based sealants. It has been known since at least the early 1980s that some silicones can behave similarly. However, this effect appears to have been encountered with greater frequency in recent years, possibly because certain formulation/substrate combinations have become more common. It may also occur with some polyurethanes, acrylics and polysulfides.

Careful consideration needs to be given to the following effects, which can be unacceptably detrimental to appearance:

- relatively rapid interaction between components of the sealant system and adjacent substrates (Section 2.5)
- the influence of sealed joints on the pattern of rainwater flow over a facade (irrespective of sealant type)
- substrate staining due to seepage from the sealant – discussed in detail below.

While the seepage of sealant components that cause this substrate staining may start immediately, it generally increases in severity over months or years.

Slightly porous substrates such as marble and slate appear to be particularly vulnerable. Fluid constituents of the sealant are drawn deeply into the stone, producing a marked discoloration that cannot be removed. If the sealant is replaced, the stain may continue to spread for some years, diminishing in intensity and thus becoming less obvious. Solvent cleaning (or heating) may similarly reduce the intensity while not removing the stain. Special treatments for this type of staining are becoming available, but their use usually requires the involvement of the manufacturer.

Seepage staining has also been observed on granite, but it is reported that limestone and reconstructed stone are seldom affected.

Appropriate primers/sealers can prevent the effect; testing with exactly the same sealant and substrate used on a project is essential. Any evaluations should be carried out by or in consultation with the sealant supplier as the staining may not be reproduced under some test conditions (standard screening procedures are currently unavailable but are being developed).

Staining of non-porous substrates by some sealants is also known. Here the fluid migrates across the surface and attracts fine dust, creating an unacceptable appearance. Removal is again very difficult; special solutions may be effective but their use requires great care and experience.

There are many instances in construction where proven materials cause major problems when formulations or the circumstances of use are changed slightly; a new generation of products is then developed, as in the case of the silicone sealants that are now becoming available as 'stain-free' products.

2.10 LIFE EXPECTANCY

2.10.1 Service life claims

The figures given in Table 2.2 for generic life expectancy are not unique to this guide. Similar information commonly appears in wide-ranging literature dealing with high-performance sealants, including National Standards (BS6093: 1993).

While not doubting the validity of this data, which is supported by many case histories, the individual designer/specifier may question its usefulness – particularly when having to select a proprietary product. He will be seeking the longest sealant life, because of the prestigious nature of the building, the difficulty of providing access for remedial work, or simply the high cost of replacing perhaps 50 to 100 km of sealant.

After accepting the caveat that good design and application are essential if a quoted lifetime is to be achieved, the designer has few other useful terms of reference. More specifically, there is little, if any, information on the distribution of performance after long periods – for example, where workmanship appears to be satisfactory because premature failure has not occurred. While it may be reassuring to know that an average of 20 or more years can be achieved, the probability of attaining this service life in a particular case is usually unknown.

The factors responsible for loss of serviceability can certainly be identified. However, they cannot be quantified sufficiently well for the sensitivity of sealant systems to be defined for given circumstances. Put another way, the statement that 'under favourable conditions, the quoted life expectancy will be exceeded' begs the question concerning the specific details of *un*favourable conditions that might lead to a service life of only 15 years, rather than 25 years. This is a significant difference for buildings with a very long design life.

2.10.2 Factors contributing to uncertainty

Suppliers cannot be held responsible for the uncertainty of life expectancy discussed above. New materials can spur innovation in construction. More often, the manufacturer must meet specific challenges set by the designer and the architect, who may not fully appreciate the complexity of an apparently simple application. For joint sealing systems, the following factors, for example, contribute towards the uncertainties regarding life expectancy:

- while figures are given for generic types of sealant, they do not relate to specific products; where the latter information is available from suppliers, such case histories may not take account of formulation changes (stimulated by economic factors, the availability of components, health and safety regulations, and the general desire to improve products)
- the overall performance of sealant/primer systems is critically dependent upon adhesion being maintained over very long periods; it is increasingly difficult to ensure that this requirement will be met, due to the wide variations in substrate surface chemistry presented by building components
- many modern buildings are unique, making it difficult simply to transfer earlier experience of sealant performance; the rates and exact modes of joint movement are particularly difficult to classify
- correct application is critical and not always easy to control, particularly in climates with very rapidly varying weather conditions

- in comparison with some traditional construction materials, synthetic polymers degrade by complex mechanisms and the influence of even common factors is difficult to predict and quantify
- sealant performance depends upon the interaction of a number of properties: adhesion, the long-term response to a varying strain condition, tolerance of stress concentrations and resistance to the degrading effects of the weather.

There is no simple solution to the problem of predicting service life with more assurance. Longer experience and greater understanding of the fundamental mechanisms controlling degradation will, with time, assist – as will further development of test procedures giving results that may reliably be extrapolated to service environments. Other approaches may also be utilised to a greater degree, e.g., empirical predictive models that weight each of the significant influences on performance.

As noted in BS7543: 1992, predicting durability is not an exact science and often relies upon informed estimates. This Standard, which is intended to discourage unrealistic expectations, is valuable in setting out general principles upon which more detailed assessments can be developed.

2.10.3   Premature failure and misuse

A well-formulated and installed sealant in a properly designed joint should reach the end of an acceptable service life due to the synergistic effects of joint movement and weathering. For sealants to be cost-effective, it is essential that additional factors (created by the designer, the supplier and the applicator) do not contribute towards the common types of premature failure that are summarised in Table 2.6.

Both the earlier and following sections of this guide are aimed at assisting the attainment of cost-effective use. Implicitly, the whole guide should convey that, while sealants are a seemingly minor element in the external envelope of buildings (as indeed they are in terms of initial costs), they can, when misused, become responsible for major expenditure, in addition to considerable inconvenience and internal damage. For these reasons, and because the current estimates of life expectancy are not precise design parameters, but averages with an unknown deviation, it is essential that close and informed attention is given to all the detailed aspects of sealant usage, from the early design stage onwards.

Table 2.6 *Common types of failure and their origins*

Adhesive

Poor design – inadequate MAF and/or sealant width/profile

Inadequately prepared, contaminated substrate surface (including dampness)

No/wrong primer or open time exceeded

Excessive movement (amplitude and/or frequency) for width of joint or sealant type

Poor quality (or incorrectly formulated) sealant/primer

Poor installation – usable life exceeded, ineffective tooling, etc.

Excessively wet conditions for the substrate/primer/sealant combination

Note: A failure that leaves a thin film of sealant on the substrate should be classified as cohesive failure

---

Cohesive

Poor design – inadequate MAF and/or sealant width/profile (sealant may be too deep or too shallow depending on circumstances)

Excessive movement (amplitude and/or frequency/rate)

Poor-quality sealant (or incorrectly formulated)

Poor installation – poor mixing, inadequate depth, non-uniform profile

Slow cure rate (or excessive early joint movement)

Increased hardness/shrinkage with weathering (more plastic sealant types)

Air voids – poor installation/tooling

Back-up poorly installed

Adhesion to back-up or absence of bond breaker

Miscellaneous

Spalling – weak substrate surface compared to cohesive/adhesive strength of sealant

Necking or bulging – sealant and joint movement poorly matched; incorrect sealant profile; slow cure rate

Slumping – sealant of poor quality/wrong grade; poor installation technique for wide joints

Folding – excessive movement of plastic/elasto-plastic sealant and permanent set

Substrate staining – an inappropriate combination of substrate/primer/sealant

Surface chalking, cracking, crazing – natural weathering (plus movement); some sealants more susceptible than others; complete failure may not occur

Non-uniform colour – poor mixing

Poor cure/tacky surface – poor mixing; poor ambient conditions; tooling lubricant inappropriate

Dirt pick-up – slow cure; some sealants more susceptible than others

---

2.11　MAINTENANCE AND RESEALING

2.11.1　Maintenance

Sealants should not be viewed as being routinely maintainable. With correct design and installation, a sealant should require little, if any, attention other than periodic inspection. This should be performed primarily to give warning of impending failure, particularly where significant consequential damage could occur. Useful guidance on maintenance is given in BS8210: 1986.

If unsightly fungal growths need to be removed, a cleaning method approved by the sealant supplier should be used.

Failures due to design errors, incorrect selection, poor application or unexpected movement may occur after a short service life and major resealing may be required. Minor defects are most likely to be the result of poor application or vandalism, and partial replacement with the original sealant may be possible. The exact reason for the failure must be confirmed and an assessment of whether it is likely to be progressive should be carried out (see below). Advice should be obtained from the sealant supplier regarding an appropriate method of repair (Section 5.5).

More extensive and progressive premature failure may point to a more fundamental problem; in addition to resealing, a replacement sealant possessing a higher level of performance may have to be considered.

2.11.2　Resealing

Assuming that premature failure has been avoided and that good long-term performance has been achieved, it remains likely that joints will require resealing during the lifetime of a building. This process is usually far more difficult than sealing the joints initially. Apart from the problems of access and of removing the bulk of the old sealant, the presence of sealant/primer residues has to be treated as contamination, which can be extremely difficult to remove adequately. Depending upon the specific materials involved, satisfactory adhesion of the new sealant system can then be seriously impaired for a number of reasons:

- the primer/sealant residues reduce the 'micro-roughness' of surfaces such as concrete and anodised aluminium
- it is inherently difficult to achieve good adhesion to some cured sealants due to the chemical nature of the surface, e.g., silicones, and particularly to non-curing (oleo-resinous) sealants
- sealant residues may be cohesively weak or have a very low modulus.

Consequently, there is a risk that an initially acceptable service life will be followed by premature failure, as illustrated in Figure 2.16.

In Figure 2.16, 20 years is given as an example of the average period that may be attained before resealing is necessary. Ideally, a similar service life will be achieved after resealing (Case II). However, unless all aspects of the resealing operation are correctly addressed, failure may occur after a much shorter interval (shown as five years, Case I, but possibly significantly less). This failure may generate new problems, e.g., with respect to surface preparation and adhesion. A sequence of short-term failures can then easily be encountered.

For the majority of projects, it seems unlikely that what should be distant problems connected with resealing would have a major effect on the initial selection of a sealant; for example, using a generic type that will ease future maintenance. However, an appreciation of the complexities presented by resealing operations should emphasise the need for maximising the initial service life. In some cases, maintenance may be addressed more directly at the initial design stage, for example: the primary seal may be recessed so that additional sealant can be easily installed at a later date (Section 3.5.3).

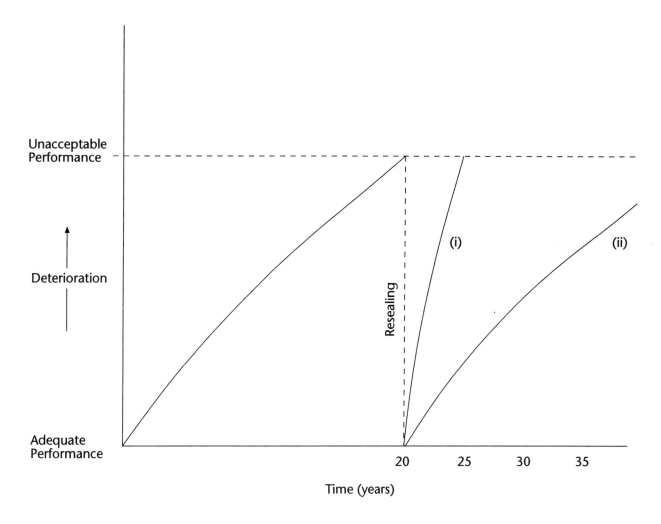

Figure 2.16 *The possible consequences of resealing following an initial acceptable service life: (i) premature failure; (ii) successful resealing*

The problem of resealing joints in buildings was addressed comprehensively in the UK by a DoE/SERC jointly funded project in the Construction, Maintenance and Refurbishment LINK programme. This collaborative project (RESEAL) was carried out between 1989 and 1992 and many of the findings have been incorporated within a book published in 1994 (Woolman and Hutchinson, 1994).

2.12 SEALANT SELECTION

2.12.1 The selection process

The provision of detailed cross-referencing showing recommended sealant types against specific location of use, as given in BS6213: 1982, was not considered desirable for this guide. Such information has to be qualified and still leaves many options. The aim here is to provide a foundation for the rational design of joints and the informed selection of sealing systems, directing attention towards the many questions that should be asked during the design/selection process. Although the answers may vary, as both the detailed needs of designers and the properties of proprietary products evolve and change with time, the key questions tend to remain constant. An understanding and familiarity with the origins of these questions is even less likely to become dated.

Figure 2.17 is provided to assist selection and to complement information provided elsewhere in this document. It gives, in the central section, various factors that are likely to be critical for most sealed joints. Key items associated with these factors are shown to the right and sources of information to the left.

Although given in the form of a flow chart, it is intended that Figure 2.17 should be used more as a check-list or review aid, particularly for those who are relatively unfamiliar with sealing systems. It should also form a bridge between the joint design procedure and the actual installation of the sealing system.

Feedback loops have been omitted for clarity, but it is anticipated that these will be necessary in most cases. Thus, a generic type considered initially on the basis of movement accommodation might be rejected if it is unsuitable for the anticipated application conditions; or, one of two otherwise acceptable proprietary products may be eliminated, on review, due to inferior resistance to weathering. Hence, as is the case with many selection tasks, there is an iterative process with the gradual elimination of unsuitable options.

This process may also be used in conjunction with detailed selection tables of the type given in BS6213: 1982. As noted in this Standard, a short-list of possibly appropriate sealant types may be derived from the tables, but it cannot be assumed that all are of equal durability and fitness for the specific purpose. The points conveyed in Figure 2.17 should assist both in reducing this short-list and then ensuring that the claims made for proprietary product options do not conflict.

2.12.2 Information inputs

The earlier contents of this section have concentrated on the factors listed on the right-hand side of Figure 2.17. However, several additional points should be made regarding the information inputs on the left-hand-side.

Consultation

The need for consultation with suppliers has been emphasised frequently. This is essential because data sheets cannot convey all the product information available or address all specific circumstances. Hence, they should be considered as an introduction to the product, conveying the information that is needed during the initial stage of the selection process. Typical information that should be given on data sheets is summarised in Table 2.7.

Table 2.7 *Information provided on sealant data sheets*

General information

Description	Generic type/cure mechanism
Colour	Range available
Consumption	Density
Shelf life	Required storage conditions
Substrates	General physical/chemical/adhesive compatibility
Typical uses	Joint types
Standards/codes/specifications	BS/ISO/ASTM, etc. complied with
Use instructions	Mixing, etc.
Failure	Typical most common causes

Application/cure properties

Temperature and humidity range	For application and cure – maximum/minimum
Joint dimensions	Maximum/minimum for application and cure
Application life and skin formation time	Under stated conditions for both extrusion and tooling
Initial cure	To tack-free state under stated conditions
Full cure	Under stated conditions (and depth)
Adhesion	Need for primer and type(s) for common substrates
	Surface dampness acceptable or not
	Problem surfaces
	New-to-old sealant adhesion

Service properties

Modulus	Tensile at stated strain and temperature
Movement accommodation factor	With definition used
Width/depth	Recommended range and limitations
Movement characteristic	Plastic/elastic etc. with figure for % recovery under stated test conditions
Temperature	Acceptable service range
Resistance	Chemicals/water
Tear resistance	
Colour/appearance	Effect of weathering
Over-painting	Yes/no with general advice and caveats
Service-life	As normally expected (with known history)

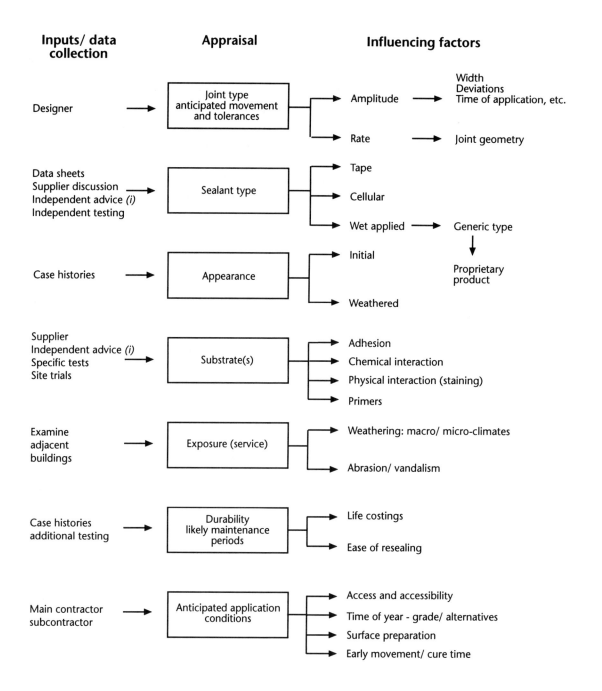

Inputs/ data collection	Appraisal	Influencing factors

Designer → Joint type anticipated movement and tolerances
→ Amplitude → Width / Deviations / Time of application, etc.
→ Rate → Joint geometry

Data sheets / Supplier discussion / Independent advice (i) / Independent testing → Sealant type
→ Tape
→ Cellular
→ Wet applied → Generic type ↓ Proprietary product

Case histories → Appearance
→ Initial
→ Weathered

Supplier / Independent advice (i) / Specific tests / Site trials → Substrate(s)
→ Adhesion
→ Chemical interaction
→ Physical interaction (staining)
→ Primers

Examine adjacent buildings → Exposure (service)
→ Weathering: macro/ micro-climates
→ Abrasion/ vandalism

Case histories / additional testing → Durability likely maintenance periods
→ Life costings
→ Ease of resealing

Main contractor / subcontractor → Anticipated application conditions
→ Access and accessibility
→ Time of year - grade/ alternatives
→ Surface preparation
→ Early movement/ cure time

Notes:
(i) 'Independent advice' includes codes, British Board of Agrement and specialist consultants, etc.
(ii) Feedback loops occur throughout - refer to text.

Figure 2.17   *The selection of a sealant*

Standards

Reference on data sheets to compliance with national standards or codes of practice can be informative and beneficial to the designer/specifier, provided, of course, that the standard itself addresses his real needs. Unfortunately, standards often deal with short-term properties and testing, which is closely related to quality control. Hence, they give no reassurance regarding long-term performance.

Standards can also be too broad. When this is the case, compliance is not an adequate specification for the sealant as it may encompass individual products with considerable differences. For example, sealants formulated mainly for civil engineering applications may be quite different to those produced for the building envelope, although both comply with the same national standard. Uninformed specification or selection, solely on the basis of compliance, may then lead to premature failure.

International standards, currently being developed and drafted, should assist in resolving these difficulties as they will provide performance classifications that are more closely related to certain end-uses (see, for example, Section 2.8.2), in addition to focusing more closely on durability.

2.12.3 Proprietary product selection

Early confirmation of a specific proprietary product, or, at least, the listing of just a few alternatives, is required for a number of the potential inputs shown in Figure 2.17, e.g., additional testing, site trials, mock-ups, etc. This may not be possible when a performance specification has been issued and a specialist subcontractor is appointed close to the time of installing the sealant. In such cases, the applicator's preference may well determine the actual product that is used.

Increasingly throughout the EU, the Construction Products Directive and related legislation is requiring products to be specified on a performance basis rather than by name. Consequently, it may be necessary to appoint the sealant applicator at an early stage when pre-installation assessment is considered to be necessary. Apart from the benefits of testing, etc., this would allow potential installation problems to be resolved, e.g., lack of joint accessibility, agreement of suitable weather conditions, etc. Method statements could also be agreed and benchmarks for workmanship set (Section 5.2.2).

2.12.4 Site conditions and records

The application conditions found on site, and even those applicable to service, are often more severe than envisaged during design and specification. The implicit safety margins given by the good design of sealed joints may thus be lowered, both by these factors and, also, by adequate, but less than perfect, workmanship. This is particularly true with regard to surface preparation, for example, where there are few objective criteria. In some cases, therefore, it may be advisable to reduce the risks of failure further by specifying a higher-performance sealing system than that suggested by conventional good design. Compared to the likely cost of remedial work, any additional materials cost is likely to be of a relatively small order. However, a contractor considering this approach would have to ensure that the provisional sums used in his tender are adequate.

Finally, although not providing an input to the selection process, it is recommended that stipulations regarding detailed site records should be given in the specification for a sealing system. If failure does occur, whether prematurely or after a longer service period, such records are an invaluable aid to resealing joints effectively (Sections 3.6 and 5.2.1).

2.12.5   Future developments

The conventional method of selection discussed above is usually a complex and time-consuming process, as a multitude of performance parameters needs to be considered. Errors can result in remedial costs that considerably exceed those of the initial installation. More generally, the selection of materials for many industrial applications has always presented a problem, and it is one that is becoming increasingly complicated as new product variations are introduced.

In several areas at least – plastics and adhesives, for example – the process has been assisted by computerised databases that, over the past 10 to 15 years have been developed into knowledge-based expert systems for selection. This approach has been introduced in North America for joint sealants (Lacasse, Thomas and Woolsey, 1994). This system has been developed to support the design of joints in new construction by providing a systematic method for the selection of proprietary products and the generation of complete specification documents.

3   Principles of design of joints with sealants

The aim of this section is to provide a guide to the broad principles involved in design of sealant joints. Section 1 provides an overall strategy. Section 2 provides full details of the materials selection process required for identification of an appropriate sealant. Section 4 will expand on the principles of joint design outlined in this section to use them in schematic examples of joints on buildings. Section 5 addresses installation.

3.1   BACKGROUND TO DESIGN OF SEALANT JOINTS

3.1.1   Design responsibility

The joint design process is complex, covering such aspects as CDM Regulations and complex materials selection procedures, and requires the detailed involvement of various members of the construction 'team'. It is important that one person should accept overall responsibility for all aspects of joint design. However, confusion is likely to arise over who takes on this role of 'joint designer' (Introduction), which will vary with the size and complexity of each project. This section makes no presumption about where the responsibility for joint design lies, but outlines the factors that should be considered in the design process.

3.1.2   Purpose of joints

Joints may be present to accommodate movement (movement joints) responding to 'real' material behaviour (e.g., thermal dimensional changes) or, as in bolted joints between metallic sections, may permit little or no movement (i.e., fixed or low-movement joints) as an essential feature of the assembly process. In both cases, some sealing may be required (to preserve weathertightness, for example).

Joints will:

- require good design (consideration of movements/tolerances, etc.)
- make good detailing essential
- require good workmanship to match design parameters
- influence building appearance
- influence water flow on the facade
- present a potential risk to the building owners (in terms of, for example, unauthorised entry, vandalism, maintenance commitment)

Joints should only be provided after careful consideration of both the reasons for their use and their expected role.

As already outlined in Section 1, a joint may be defined as a discontinuity between similar or dissimilar components in the building envelope. The joint may then need to be sealed in order to meet certain design factors (e.g., weathertightness) in addition to certain material considerations (e.g., durability). Effective design of this seal will strike a compromise between the many needs of a particular joint. It may also take account of particular essential performance requirements (Section 1.5) on a case by case basis, such as:

- resistance/barrier to insects/vermin
- acceptable appearance avoiding weathering, discoloration, dust collection, mould/plant growth
- resistance to vandalism.

It is rare that such factors will be needed in isolation. The designer will have to compromise to obtain the best balance between conflicting requirements. In addition, the designer may have to consider such aspects as:

- ease of initial installation and subsequent maintenance/replacement (Sections 3.5.3 and 5.5)
- environmental impact (Sections 2.5.6 and 3.1.7)
- potential risk/hazard during installation (Sections 2.5.6 and 3.1.6).

The importance of these and other factors influencing the options for joint sealing will vary. Shielding to protect from UV, for example, could be important for both fixed and movement joints throughout their life. Flexibility, or movement accommodation, however, will generally be important only at installation for fixed joints (in order to accommodate tolerances or lack of fit), but throughout the building life for movement joints (in order to cope with movement).

When considering the type and size of joint to be used, the following questions need to be asked:

- why   -   Why is a joint required?
              Why do we need to seal it?

- where -   Where is the joint located?

- what   -   What performance requirements are to be satisfied?
              What movements will need to be accommodated?
              What deviations are likely?
              What material should be used in the joint?
              What are the consequences of premature failure?

- how   -   How should the joint be designed?
              How is the selected material specified and applied?
              How is it inspected/maintained/replaced should it fail?

While the ultimate goal of a totally sealed building envelope may seem desirable, it is not the only option; open joints can be a very effective design solution (provided, of course, potential problems of water penetration are dealt with by other means, Section 4).

3.1.3   Sealed joint options

The answers to the above four questions naturally create a range of possible solutions. There is often a choice between open or sealed joints, and between different methods of sealing joints. If joints are to be sealed, there is a choice between:

- sealant, where the material is applied to the joint in an uncured state

- gaskets, where a cured polymeric material is compressed into a joint to form a seal
- cellular sealing strips, where foam material is compressed into the joint to form a seal (Section 2.2)
- mastic sealing strips, where a soft, synthetic rubber is compressed into a joint (Section 2.1.2)
- baffles, which may act as protection in an open joint (e.g., strip in open drained joint).

Checks to avoid recognised weaknesses of sealants in joints include:

- whether the correct amount of material for the joint size and depth has been installed
- whether the quality of workmanship on site is acceptable (e.g., have two-part sealants been mixed adequately?)
- whether the correct sealant system has been specified, used or applied.

Gaskets are preformed seals that are installed in joints to provide a compression seal. Therein lies the key difference between sealants and gaskets. Sealants will generally be fluctuating between tension and compression, whereas gaskets should generally be working in various states of compression to ensure they continue to seal the joint. For a gasket to provide any sealing capability in tension it must be fixed to the adjacent moving component in some way (e.g., as in the use of sealing 'bandages' over expansion joints). Sealing strips are a type of gasket and are discussed further in Sections 2.2 and 3.2.5.

Wet-applied sealants can vary considerably in terms of both composition and performance. Sealants could be used to solve problems ranging from joints between largely fixed units to a fully engineered sealant capable of accommodating a range of movements.

Types of joint in the building envelope can be broadly classified into two categories:

- essentially fixed, 'low-movement' joints, where accommodation of deviations between elements is more important in design than accommodation of large movements
- 'high-movement' joints, where tolerance of movement is an additional key factor in design.

The design approaches naturally differ between the two joint types.

For 'fixed' joints, considerations such as accommodation of deviations (Section 3.4), durability and adhesion dominate (Section 2.4 and 2.5) and low-performance sealants (Section 2.1) or sealing strips (Sections 2.2 and 3.2.5) may be capable of providing adequate performance. Alternatively, the designer may choose to use a higher-performance sealant to provide superior adhesion, durability or flexibility in the joint. As movement is small, less 'flexible' joint geometries are sometimes used to ensure adequate sealant depth for weatherproofing (Section 3.2.1).

For high-movement joints, the ability of a sealant to accommodate movement must be addressed alongside the factors outlined in Section 2. The aim of Section 3 is to outline how sealant joints can be designed for movement, in addition to outlining additional factors (including some Regulations) that may influence good joint design.

3.1.4   Design strategy: designing for movement

Movement in buildings must be accommodated. The designer may choose one of two options:

1.   To limit movement (e.g., by coating to prevent excessive moisture movement or to fix the joint and size members to accommodate induced stresses or even to change originally proposed materials, if practical).

2.   To provide suitable joints and connections at appropriate locations to accommodate predicted movements.

If movement has not been taken into account, the building may create its own joints by cracking. These cracks will inevitably be unplanned, unsightly and unwelcome, and a separate materials selection process to seal such cracks may be required.

In general, designers will choose one of the options above. For reinforced concrete, for example, this could come down to incorporation of considerable reinforcement to resist cracking under a range of movements, or provision of regularly spaced joints, requiring much reduced reinforcement. For many structures, designers should be aware that fixings (e.g., of cladding to frame) can also permit or control movement. Movements can often be restrained in one location and be accommodated elsewhere. This subject is addressed in more detail in BRE Digest 223, BS8297: 1995 and BS8298: 1994.

There are no hard and fast rules as to the location and number of joints required. Indeed, different frequencies and sizes of joints may well be required on different aspects of buildings. Significant issues will include:

*   properties of materials involved
*   environmental conditions (e.g., temperature ranges)
*   overall building dimensions
*   appearance
*   desirability of avoiding complex joint intersections
*   construction considerations (storey heights, joints between walls/windows, changes of building shape/height, change in form of construction, change in ground conditions, etc.).

Typical joint spacings for common building materials are given in Section 3.3.5.

It is critical for joints in the structural frame to carry through to any facade elements or finishes. If they do not, cracking in the facade or finishes is almost inevitable. The reverse is, however, not necessarily true; facades (since they will be directly exposed to the elements while the frame is shielded by insulation, etc.) will generally require many more joints than the structure itself. Successful design team interaction (e.g., between designers of fabric, finishes, structure and services) is essential to ensure that joints in the frame, envelope and services are co-ordinated.

3.1.5   Design strategy: designing for variability

In addition to designing for movement, it is recognised that buildings and building components are never formed exactly to the design dimensions; allowance for deviations in both manufacture and construction must always be made. This subject is addressed further in Section 3.4 – Deviations. Estimated variability for different materials and forms of construction are outlined in Section 1.

In principle, the designer has two broad options:

1. Select joint details to accommodate expected variability and accept characteristic accuracy (i.e., have joint details that can cope with variability).

2. Where joints cannot accommodate expected variability, specify tighter, but achievable, tolerances, or make a fundamental design change if the detail still cannot accommodate variability (i.e., by increasing the frequency of joints).

Characteristic accuracy can be achieved by 'normal' labour using 'normal' methods under 'normal' conditions. These parameters will produce a predictable level of accuracy for a particular method of construction (BS5606: 1990 gives more details).

Specified accuracy will require special workmanship, methods or conditions and so may incur increased labour cost. This will be justified only if a special production plant or other onerous circumstances are present (e.g., precise installation of production equipment). The designer should be reasonable, however. There is no justification for requesting unnecessary levels of accuracy at significant cost to the client if a more 'tolerant' joint detail could have solved the problem.

Having specified the accuracy, however, it is important to carry out checks for likely 'fit' between the building components on site (BRE Digest 199). Once realistic accuracy requirements have been selected and designed (as outlined in the appropriate Codes, e.g., concrete BS8110, steel BCSA/SCI 203/91, precast concrete cladding BS8297: 1995, stone cladding BS8298: 1994 and BS5390: 1976, brick/block masonry BS5628: Pt 3), a check should be made as to whether they are achieved in practice.

3.1.6 CDM (Construction Design and Management) Regulations

The CDM Regulations, in force since April 1995, place onerous requirements on many people (including the designer) to take particular care in the selection of any material or construction process. Among other requirements, the designer must:

1. Ensure that the design takes account of the need to avoid foreseeable health and safety risks to those persons building, maintaining, repairing, cleaning, or demolishing the structure and to those affected by this work.

2. Combat at source the above risks.

The implications of CDM on the design of joints have yet to be fully assessed, but the Regulations may influence significantly both design options and method of assembly. Joint selection should aim to minimise risk to operatives during installation, sealant removal and replacement. Access for installation should be considered and exposure to harmful components and hazardous processes should be minimised. Similarly, limiting the number of operations (e.g., use of sealants that can adhere without a primer) may limit the time spent on the scaffold on the outside of a tall office block. Any potential hazard associated with sealant installation is, then, slightly reduced.

It may be appropriate, for example, to also consider the choices between:

*   sealant or gasket type joint
*   sealant removal/replacement internally or replacement via cradle/scaffold

- easy sealant removal/replacement or sealant removal/joint grinding/replacement (resealing may create more problems and risks than initial installation)
- hazardous curing mechanism or non-hazardous.

Access both for construction and maintenance will be an important consideration. Areas of difficult access (e.g., over a street where maintenance could be problematic) could be sealed with materials of greater durability. Where it is possible to select a 'safer' material or process, this should be carefully considered, but, if this is not practicable, it is essential to minimise exposure to harmful elements. In general, the CDM Regulations aim to promote selection of the most appropriate material (in terms of both performance and health and safety) for a particular application, applied with minimal risk. Initial material selection, installation and life cycle (thus including removal, disposal and replacement) are included in the risk assessment.

More detailed information can be found in publications of the Health and Safety Executive and *CDM Regulations – Case Study Guidance for Designers: An Interim Report,* by CIRIA.

3.1.7 Environmental impact

For use of sealants in the building envelope, there is clearly a 'scale effect' of environmental impact that could be taken into account. While concrete and steel, for example, are used in very large volumes, sealants form a relatively small portion of the total volume of building materials in use, with consequent reduction in relative environmental impact. In addition, there can be clear benefits resulting from the use of sealants, not least from their ability to keep the elements out of buildings!

While it may be desirable to categorise construction materials into high, medium, or low environmental impacts, such distinctions are difficult, if not impossible, to make at present in the absence of a standardised approach. The perceived environmental impact of a material critically depends on the method of assessment adopted, and the result obtained will vary according to whether, say, embodied energy (cradle to grave), pollution effects or some other measure of environmental impact is used as the primary method of assessment.

The overall environmental impact of sealants may be less than initial evidence would suggest (Section 2.5.6). However, the environmentally conscious specifier may think it appropriate to minimise the number of joints or to consider open joints.

3.2 OPTIMISATION OF MATERIAL PROPERTIES FOR SEALANTS

Section 2 of this document reviews materials selection for sealants in some detail. As the joint design is carried out, the material selection process will run in parallel to some extent, overlapping with design at various points. As such, this section outlines those aspects of sealant materials of particular relevance to the joint designer as joint width is calculated.

3.2.1 Shape of sealant joints

Most sealant joints in service are fitted with wet-applied sealants, although sealing strips may also be used (Sections 2.2 and 3.2.5). In order to ensure optimum sealant flexibility to accommodate movements in service, it is vital to have the correct sealant shape in the joint (Section 2.8). The force necessary to extend or compress a sealant joint will be directly related to its (installed) thickness. Too deep a joint will create resistance to movement and may increase the risk of failure. Conversely, too shallow a joint may risk concentrating movement over too small a sealant depth (increasing risk of failure) or may provide inadequate bond area or inadequate resistance to weathering.

The optimal sealant shape will provide adequate bond area to substrates, yet impart minimal stress to the sealant as the joint moves. As the depth of sealant is increased relative to joint width, the movement capability of the joint is decreased. In addition, a given movement will create an increased stress on the sealed joint.

Three joint types are commonly specified:

- butt joints (primarily acting in tension/compression)
- lap joints (primarily acting in shear)
- fillet joints (working in a combination of tension/compression/shear).

Typical joint configurations for each are shown in Figure 3.1.

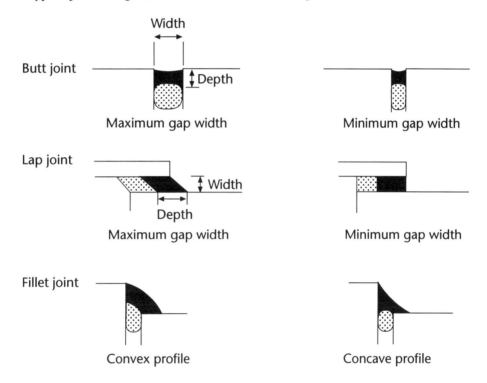

Figure 3.1 *Joint types*

The ability of a given sealant to accommodate movements is always related to the installed, not specified, joint width and depth. If the sealant bead is too narrow, the movement capability will be limited, and the sealant could fail in service. To ensure installation of the correct sealant width and shape on site, some allowance of expected deviation is critical to successful design, followed by inspection during installation. Such concepts are discussed further in Sections 2.8, 3.5.1 and 5.2.3.

Butt joints

Butt joints between ideally parallel and flush joint sides are readily accessible for installation, inspection, maintenance and replacement. On the other hand, their ability to accommodate joint deviations is limited, and any variations in joint width are conspicuous from one joint to the next. Out-of-plane components can lead to variations in joint depth that may result in failure. Their exposed nature also leaves them vulnerable to vandal attack.

Most sealant geometries used in construction tend to be butt (tension) joints, primarily due to their ease of initial sealing and ongoing maintenance. On this basis, various rules have been developed for successful performance of butt joints, subject to movement.

Preferred installed width/depth ratios vary for each type of sealant: elastic, elasto-plastic, plasto-elastic and plastic (Section 2.8.2). Typical values are shown in Table 3.1 (minimum installed depth normally 6mm).

Table 3.1 *Typical width:depth ratios for different sealant types*

Sealant type	Normal guideline W:D ratio	Maximum depth (mm)
Elastic	2:1	20
Elasto-plastic	2:1 to 1:1	20
Plasto-elastic	1:1 to 1:2	20
Plastic	1:1 to 1:3	25
Where	D = joint depth W = joint width	

Note: Joints containing sealants of predominantly plastic character that are not required to accommodate movement (or moving slowly) may go from 1:1 width:depth ratio to as much as 1:3 width:depth. Such geometries will be far less capable of accommodating movement, but help to ensure sufficient sealant depth in low-movement joints to ensure a durable weather seal (Section 2.8.3).

The tooling of butt joints against (generally) circular backing rods tends to produce concave top and bottom surfaces rather than a truly rectangular joint. This maximises the adhesive area to the joint sides, yet minimises the 'bulk' of sealant present to resist movement. In this way, it provides the ideal geometry for butt joints subject to movement (Section 2.8.2 and Figure 2.13).

Joints on a bevelled section may be used in preference to butt joints in, for example, precast concrete construction. They form a means of disguising variations of joint width (changes in width over 'x' on Figure 3.2 are far less visible than those changes over 'y'). Joints on a bevelled section also reduce the risk of damage to arrises during manufacture and handling. If the joint cannot be made wide enough to incorporate a butt (tension) joint, the convex fillet seal solution can be adopted (possible), provided the rules for fillet joint design are followed.

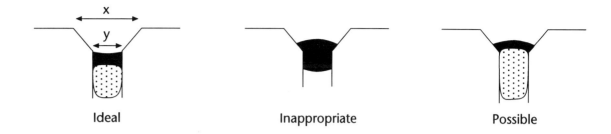

Figure 3.2 *Joint on a bevelled section*

Lap (shear) joints

Lap (or shear) joints are generally capable of accommodating more movement than can a sealant working in tension (depending on relative joint depths and tensile/shear properties of the sealant). A lap joint can shear before sealant application without changing the joint width (Figure 3.1). As the sealant is shielded from direct weathering, durability can be enhanced significantly. Lap joints also allow deviations to be disguised at joints with ease and are well suited to, for example, horizontal joints in cladding panels. Unfortunately, difficulties in cleaning, priming, installing, inspecting and replacing lap joints mean they are less successful in service than may be anticipated. Sealing strips in such applications are easier to install and can perform well (Section 2.2). Sealing new lap joints and resealing them requires care as the operative cannot see the rear face of the front element to either clean or prime.

For sealant lap joints the optimum configuration is width $\geq$ depth, where width and depth are defined as in Figure 3.1 (the joint width is the dimension perpendicular to the direction of joint movement, assuming that the joint sides move parallel to each other). When this holds, the ability of a lap joint to accommodate movement is maximised and, for a given width:depth ratio, they will cope with greater movement than butt joints. Sealants in lap joints are, however, subject to the same minimum adhesion depth requirements as butt joints and also normally require rectangular back-up rods to ensure the optimum (rectangular, parallel-sided) joint shape. For fixed lap joints, the sealant depth may be increased relative to joint width in order to ensure a weatherseal. For such joints, consideration of expected deviations, adhesion to joint sides and durability will dominate.

Overall, while lap joints offer many advantages in principle, they provide many difficulties in design and installation. As such, sealant manufacturers should be consulted for further guidance in each case.

Fillet joints

Fillet joints can be useful, particularly where the close proximity of adjacent components precludes proper application of a butt joint. Alternatively, properly designed fillet joints can be used to good effect for resealing butt joints where removal of the original sealant is particularly difficult (Figure 3.3).

a)

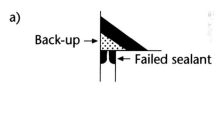

b)

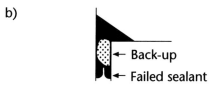

Figure 3.3 *Resealing with fillet joints*

As with butt and lap joints, fillet joints need the correct shape and size of sealant in combination with bond breakers to perform successfully. In Figure 3.3(b), the 'bulk' of sealant installed acts as a considerable barrier to movement. To maximise movement, the use of diagonal geometry backing rods that omit the sealant at the root of the fillet would be preferred, as shown in Figure 3.3(a).

The resultant theoretical geometry of sealant would take up part of its movement in shear (i.e., such that the fillet acts between a pure tension butt joint and a pure shear lap joint).

Unfortunately, backer rods of such geometry are not widely available, and such 'optimal' use of fillet joints is rare.

In reality, most fillet seals have weak capacity, are vulnerable to vandalism and are over used. Fillet seals should therefore be avoided for high-movement joints. Fillet joints are, however, still widely used in certain low-movement applications (e.g., window installation). Where used, the sealant should ideally be applied such that it is at least 6 mm thick, with at least 6 mm bite onto the adjacent surfaces.

Where there is a gap greater than 5 mm between adjoining faces, a bond breaker/backing material should be inserted. Fillet seals may be concave or convex. For convex seals the bond breaker/back-up rod shall be placed as shown in Figure 3.4(a). For concave seals the bond breaker/back-up rod shall be placed to achieve the geometry shown in Figure 3.4(b). The aim is to place the sealant in a shape where the throat of the seal is thinner than the bite onto each of the adjacent surfaces while preventing adhesion to the base of the joint. This reduces the risk of adhesive failure.

Concave seals are easier to tool. Convex seals accommodate greater movement and perform better if properly made. Concave seals are most commonly used, but if the dimensions given in Figure 3.4 are not used, there may be failure as shown in Figure 3.5. If the edges of a concave seal are feathered, localised weathering deterioration may occur. For these reasons the use of shear or butt joints is preferable to fillet joints where possible.

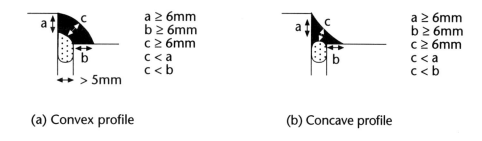

a ≥ 6mm
b ≥ 6mm
c ≥ 6mm
c < a
c < b

> 5mm

a ≥ 6mm
b ≥ 6mm
c ≥ 6mm
c < a
c < b

(a) Convex profile   (b) Concave profile

Figure 3.4 *Fillet seals*

Peeling

Tearing

Figure 3.5 *Failure of fillet seals*

3.2.2   Back-up materials and joint fillers

A typical sealant joint may comprise a number of important components: the primer, the sealant, the back-up material, debonding strip or bond breaker and the joint filler. (Section 2.3) In order to ensure the correct installed geometry of sealant in a joint, back-up materials are essential. The purpose of such materials is discussed further in Sections 2.3.1 and 2.3.2.

Joint fillers can be used to help form joints prior to sealant installation and are often retained in the joint in the final works to provide support to the sealant, to exclude debris that could block joint faces and possibly to improve fire/sound/thermal performance. Such materials may contain bitumen or other components that create potential incompatibility problems with the sealant material. They may promote bond and so should generally be separated from the final seal.

Joint fillers may also be incompressible. For fired-clay products, where expansion is a predominant feature, use of stiff joint fillers can allow direct transmission of load through the joint on closure and so should be avoided in all such cases (Table 3.2). BS5628 suggests a pressure of about 0.1 N/mm^2 should be sufficient to compress joint fillers in fixed clay brickwork to 50% of their original thickness. The use of hemp, fibreboard, cork and similar materials in these situations should be avoided.

Once a joint has been formed, the sealant must be installed in the correct shape, and at the correct width-to-depth ratio to ensure optimum performance. It is important to ensure that the optimum geometry can be obtained (by checking depth of seal before/after installation), whether the sealant would adhere to the filler board (if present) and whether compatibility with the filler board is of concern. In general, a backing strip/debonding tape would be required (which may be an inert closed-cell foam or a tape). This is located immediately before installation of the sealant.

Table 3.2 *Fillers for movement joints (from BS6093)*

Joint filler type	Property Typical uses	Form	Density range kg/m³	Pressure for 50% compression N/mm²	Resilience (recovery after compression) %	Tolerance to water immersion
Wood fibre/ bitumen	General-purpose expansion joints	Sheet, strip	200–400	0.7–5.2	70–85	Not suitable
Bitumen/cork	General-purpose expansion joints	Sheet	500–600	0.7–5.2	70–80	Suitable
Cork/resin	Expansion joints in water-retaining structures where bitumen is not acceptable*	Sheet, strip	200–300	0.5–3.4	85–95	Suitable
Cellular plastics and rubbers	Low-load transfer joints	Sheet, strip	40–60	0.07–0.34	85–95	Suitable
Mineral or ceramic fibres, or intumescent strips	Fire-resistant joints: low movement	Loose fibre or braided and strip	Dependent upon degree of compaction	Dependent upon degree of compaction	Slight	Not suitable

* Note: Depending on the product selected, and the degree of exposure to water, some risk of failure may be present.

3.2.3   Visco-elastic properties

Comparing the predicted rate and type of building movements with the capabilities of any proposed sealant is important (Sections 1.5.4 and 2.7.4).

As outlined in Section 2.7.4, sealant materials can be classified into elastic, elasto-plastic, plasto-elastic and plastic characteristics. While elastic sealants, for example, exhibit excellent recovery after movement, their ability to show stress relaxation (the gradual decay of an applied stress at given strain) is limited. Elasto-plastic sealants, however, show reasonable elasticity within a constant fluctuating joint, yet have the ability to stress-relieve under permanent deformation and then demonstrate good elasticity in the new geometry.

Hence, in a structure where deformations lead to a permanent opening or closing of a joint, an elastic sealant may be more prone to failure than, say, an elasto-plastic sealant. Conversely, in a structure of joints subject to rapidly fluctuating movements, an elastic sealant may be more appropriate.

Plastic sealants are capable of considerable stress relaxation accompanied by change of geometry. This may, however, result in adhesive failure of the sealant if permanent opening joint movements become excessive.

3.2.4 Stresses within the sealant in a joint

The performance of a sealant in a joint will depend on conditions while curing. If a joint is sealed when the joint is at its narrowest, the tensile strain would be maximised. Conversely, if the joint is sealed when at the maximum specified joint width, the subsequent tensile strain is reduced (since, when the temperature is low, subsequent movements tend to close the joint). Selection of the latter time for sealing is generally preferred (provided, of course, the sealant does not bulge excessively from the joint when it closes).

Selection of both joint geometry and sealant type will influence the stresses within the sealant in a joint. The stresses induced in a lap joint subject to movement may be as little as half that (for the same movement and width:depth ratio) in a butt joint. The force exerted on the sealant joint line will increase as the sealant depth increases for a given joint movement. In addition, the modulus of a sealant can be related to the likelihood of adhesive failure; for a given strain, higher-modulus sealants will create greater forces on the joint line than low-modulus materials (i.e., 'stiff' sealants become more highly stressed for a given movement than 'flexible' ones).

Although many materials possess excellent movement capability in principle, the translational force required to produce such deformation can be considerable. For a heavily filled epoxy polysulfide sealant, for example, it may be possible to accommodate 50% compression in the joint, but a stress of some 14 N/mm^2 may be required to produce this deformation. The effect of this stress in producing a resultant force on adjacent building elements (e.g., masonry) should not be overlooked, and care in specifying an appropriate sealant type to reduce such forces is required.

3.2.5 Preformed sealing strips

(Sections 2.1.2 and 2.2.)

Sealing strips are a particular form of gasket (i.e., they are applied to joints as a preformed seal as opposed to wet-applied sealants). They typically comprise either open-cell foams that have been impregnated (e.g., by bitumen) or 'mastic strips', which provide weathertightness when compressed into a joint. They do not normally rely on adhesion to the joint sides for performance, but will continue to provide joint sealing properties provided they are compressed within their operating range. The reaction is not chemical, but purely physical through pressure against the sides of the joint. The primary advantages of sealing strips include:

- predictable depth of seal
- predictable properties if properly compressed (since the product is preformed).

With cellular sealing strips it is important to ensure that the correct type of strip is installed. The strip is compressed into the joint width at the time of sealing and will continue to seal only if the joint does not subsequently move beyond certain dimensions. It is, however, comparatively easy to check that joint dimensions are acceptable before installation and, if necessary, to change to a larger-section strip with appropriate subsequent movement capability. In this way, use of this family of materials may still successfully solve problems of tapering joints, although the creation of a butt joint between the two strip sections may act as an inherent weakness.

Key factors to note with sealing strips (Section 2.2) include:

- relationship of compression to quality of seal (depending on type of product selected and degree of compression, the open-cell nature of the cellular strip may permit some fluid penetration)
- chemical resistance of cellular strip within a joint will be dependent on temperature
- rate of expansion of cellular strip within a joint will be dependent on temperature
- joint intersections are simple butt joint connections.

Several types of sealing strips are available, some with British Board of Agrément approval. Overall, manufacturers' guidance is an essential tool for selection of sealing strip in relation to type of joint, and the strip manufacturer should be consulted as part of the materials selection process.

3.3 MOVEMENT

Sections 1.5 and 1.6 provided an overview of both the causes and approach to estimation of movements for various components in the building envelope. The aim of this section is to provide further background to the considerations and calculations required for a realistic assessment of movement at a joint.

3.3.1 Sources of movement

In order to produce an accurate prediction of the likely movement at a joint, it is important to reflect on the key factors influencing that movement. In general, materials will move due to one or more of the following:

- thermal movements (expansion on temperature rise, contraction as temperature falls)
- reversible moisture movements, relating to changes in moisture content of a building material in service
- irreversible moisture movements, relating to permanent changes in moisture content following manufacture (e.g., shrinkage of cementitious materials, moisture expansion of some fired clays)
- building movements due to loading (e.g., floor, wind, snow, settlement, heave, seismic)
- creep.

The causes of movement for particular materials are also outlined in Sections 1.5 and 1.6.

The way in which a joint responds to movement will be influenced by the materials that create the joint and the way in which they respond to the above causes. Movements will vary in terms of:

- frequency (e.g., long-term joint movement due to creep and frequent short term movements due to temperature changes)
- rate (e.g., rapid response times with aluminium cladding and slow for precast concrete)
- magnitude (dictated by material properties of components adjacent to the joint and magnitude of 'causes')
- direction (overall effect of above factors could create positive or negative movement or both)

When considering the selection of materials to seal a joint, consideration should be given to both cause and effect of any movements present. The overall movement (whether opening or closing), frequency of cycles, and rate of movement should be carefully assessed, and a sealant selected that can best cope with the movements and environmental exposure identified.

Difficulties frequently arise at the intersection between different materials. It is likely that differing characteristics of materials (e.g., modulus, thermal movement, shrinkage, expansion) will always concentrate problems at junctions, and movement joints are often required at these locations.

The design of sealant joints normally assumes that movement is smooth, gradual and unrestrained. There are some situations (e.g., build-up of force on bearings) where a so-called 'slip-stick' condition may be created – a sudden transfer of force may lead to a dynamic loading effect and greater movement than that occurring from a gradual transfer. Selection of fixings/bearings that operate with minimal restraint is the key to avoiding this effect and its potential effect on sealant joints.

3.3.2   Prediction of thermal movements

Linear changes in material dimension due to changes in temperature can be calculated directly from:

$$\Delta L = L \, \alpha \, T$$

where
ΔL = change of size
L = length of dimension
T = temperature change
α = coefficient of thermal expansion (BRE Digest 228)

Typical service temperature ranges are listed on Table 3.3, and coefficients of thermal expansion on Table 3.4 (Section 1.6.1).

Table 3.3   *Service temperature ranges for the UK (BRE Digest 228)*

Material	Colour	Min °C	Max °C	Range °C
Heavyweight	Light	-20	50	70
Heavyweight	Dark	-20	65	85
Lightweight insulated	Light	-25	60	85
Lightweight	Dark	-25	80	105

Table 3.4 *Common material properties (BRE Digest 228)*

Material	Coefficient of thermal expansion α (per °C x 10^{-6})	Modulus of elasticity (kN/mm^2)
Natural stone	3–12	3–80
Lightweight concrete	8–12	8
Dense concrete	12–14	15–36
Brick	6–12	4–25
Carbon steel	12	210
Aluminium	24	70
Zinc	23 or 33	140 or 220
Austenitic stainless steel	18	200
Lead	30	14
Wood	4–6 with grain 30–70 across grain	5–20
Phenolic boards	30–45	5–9
PVC-U	40–70	2–4
Glass	9–11	70

If contraction or expansion is restrained, the resultant stress in a component can be calculated from:

$$\sigma = \alpha\, E\, T$$

where
σ = stress
α = coefficient of thermal expansion
E = modulus of elasticity
T = change in temperature

Typical values of modulus of elasticity are given in Table 3.3.

Hence for a 20 m long flint gravel aggregate concrete panel subject to a 35°C change in temperature,

$$\Delta L = (20) \times (12 \times 10^{-6}) \times 35$$
$$= 0.0084 \text{ m}$$
$$= 8.4\text{mm}$$

This assumes a worst credible situation with fully exposed members and sustained temperatures to allow full cooling.

If this change in length were restrained, it would result in a stress,

$$\sigma = (12 \times 10^{-6}) \times (30 \times 10^3) \times (35)$$
$$= 12.6 \text{ N/mm}^2$$

If such a stress were tensile and superimposed on other existing tensile stresses, a risk of cracking would be present. The level and distribution of cracking in reality would depend on the amount, form and distribution of the reinforcement within the panel.

3.3.3 Prediction of moisture movements

Changes in size due to moisture may be either one-off movements (e.g., irreversible movements such as shrinkage) or repeated movements (e.g., reversible movements due to changes in moisture content in service) (Section 1.6.2).

Percentage changes in size can be calculated from:

$$\frac{\text{factor} \times \text{dimension}}{100}$$

Where the appropriate factor may be obtained from Table 3.5.

In most cases, an additive combination of thermal and moisture movements will be over-pessimistic. The 'correct' level is a matter for engineering judgement but may best be established by estimating the size of the dominant movement and then assessing the extent to which the other mechanism would increase (or reduce) that movement. Combination of deviations is discussed further in Section 3.4.5.

Table 3.5 *Moisture movement (BRE Digest 228)*

Material	Repeated movement (%)	Initial movement (%)
General cement-based materials	0.02–0.10	0.03–0.10
Ultra-lightweight concrete	0.10–0.20	0.20–0.40
Glass-reinforced concrete	0.15–0.25	0.08
Asbestos cement	0.15–0.25	0.08
Limestone	0.01	–
Sandstone	0.07	–
Granite/marble/slate	–	–
Wood (across grain)	0.50–4.00	–
Wood (along grain)	0.05–0.10	–
Brickwork	0.02–0.06	0.02–0.09
Clay or shale brickwork	0.02	0.02–0.07 (expansion)

3.3.4 Prediction of structural movements

Following Section 1.6.3, the structural loads causing movement may be summarised as:

- floor loading
- wind sway
- snow loading
- seismic loading
- differential settlement and heave.

Such loads may give rise to an overall tension or compression or shear displacement of the joint. As such, these loads must be carefully considered in combination when designing the joint.

Table 3.6 shows typical building movements for different structural materials. Note that sway will be reduced for structures containing braced bays of shear walls.

Table 3.6 *Building structure movements (limiting deflection ratios; L = length, H = height)*

	Steel	Concrete	Timber
Beam with brittle finishes	L/360	L/360	L/360
Beam	L/200	L/300 – L/360	L/300
Cantilever	L/180		
Sway	H/300	Approx. H/300	H/300
Settlement	L/500	L/500	L/500

3.3.5 Overall effect – spacing of movement joints

Once the factors leading to movement have been considered, the designer must assess the effect of these movements on the building. How will the structure deform? Where will movement be accommodated? Can movement be distributed? Where could 'joints' be located? Will joints be subject to one or all of tension/compression/shear?

There is no definitive rule in spacing movement joints. Even short buildings may require joints at narrow spacings if extensive restraints are present. The precise frequency of joints will be dictated by both restraint to movement and form of individual structures. Typical maximum values for the spacing of movement joints for frame materials are:

- up to 50 m sections are typical for concrete
- 50 to 100 m sections are more typical for steel.

For cladding materials:

- 12 m sections are typical for fired clay, e.g., brick panels
- 5 to 7 m typical for calcium silicate
- 6 m typical for concrete masonry (BS5628: Pt 3).

It is important to distinguish the need for joints in building frames (e.g., to accommodate thermal/shrinkage/ground movements, etc.) (Section 1.1.3) from joints in cladding, where additional joints due to component assembly may be necessary.

Once it has been established that joints are required, the location and number of joints will be related to a number of key issues including not only anticipated movement, but also structural stiffness, deviations, construction methodology, size of elements, etc. (Sections 3.1.2, 3.1.3 and 3.1.4).

3.4 DEVIATIONS

Despite the best efforts of joint designer and contractor, the joint on site is always to match the joint on the design drawing (Section 1.5.2). This section aims to introduce the basic concepts of dealing with tolerances (the designer's estimation of what variability will be present on site) and deviations (variations in joint size that are actually seen on site).

3.4.1 Variations in joint width

It is important that the installed sealant width matches (with a reasonable allowance) that perceived by the designer. Selection of sealant material and likely movement capability will have been carried out assuming a particular joint width. Too narrow a joint when sealing will limit the extent to which the installed sealant joint will accommodate subsequent expansion; conversely, too wide a joint may be unacceptable aesthetically, or may allow the sealant to slump from the joint.

Differences between the designed and installed dimensions of a joint may arise due to:

1. Deviations due to dimensional changes resulting from inherent material properties such as thermal and moisture movements (inherent deviations), as described in Section 3.3.

2. Deviations due to inaccuracies in setting out, manufacture and construction (induced deviations).

There are two common design approaches to accommodation of these: allowance for these deviations at joints present for other reasons (i.e., joints present primarily for manufacture or buildability), or provision of joints at appropriate intervals specifically to allow for these deviations.

Sealants provide a better means of accommodating deviations than do gaskets, provided these variations have been considered in the initial design. The joint designer must thus consider the likely causes of deviations for the individual building. He should:

1. Assess limits for induced deviations (permissible deviations).

2. Ensure that joint dimensions on drawings reflect this likely variability (e.g., BS1192: Pt 1: 1984 suggests description of joint width as a target size with permitted deviations, e.g., 10±2 mm).

3. Check, by on-site inspection, that the real joints can accommodate dimensional deviations as intended by the designer.

The latter point is often overlooked; sealants will only accommodate those variations and movements considered in design. If on-site inspection conflicts with design expectation, some reflection on design expectations may be appropriate.

3.4.2 Reversible inherent deviations

Reversible inherent deviations (Sections 3.3.2 and 3.3.3) comprise those deviations that are cyclic and largely related to environmental conditions (e.g., related to temperature and moisture content changes or some loadings, e.g., wind and floor).

Local temperature and rainfall charts provide only an indication of the likely 'exposure' of particular building components. Colour, orientation and degree of exposure/shelter of a particular joint may locally vary the influence of climatic conditions.

The air temperature, for example, may vary by only 45°C (-5°C to 40°C), but surface temperatures may reach 80°C and fall to -20°C, given certain combinations of material and exposure factors (Section 1.6.1 and BRE Digest 228). In addition, surface and temperatures may differ markedly – a cold but sunny day could still produce an extremely high surface temperature on a dark surface due to absorption of radiant energy. Furthermore, mean body temperatures may differ from surface temperature, depending on the thermal conductivity and degree of thermal isolation of the element.

The rate at which a given component responds to temperature will be influenced by:

- exposure/orientation
- response to thermal change
- degree of thermal isolation and thermal mass (e.g., rapid movement of an insulated aluminium panel as against slow response of a precast concrete unit)
- colour of surface
- presence of restraint to movement.

While a designer can, for example, make allowance for overall thermal movement on the basis of typical thermal expansion coefficients, these figures may have to be confirmed for individual components on site. Specification of an acceptable 'surface temperature' at application should be considered (Section 1.6.1).

Moisture variations may be a significant influence on, for example, concrete blockwork, timber and sandstone cladding units. For sandstone and timber, the in-situ movement may even exceed that attributable to thermal variations (Section 1.6.2).

Moisture movements may be minimised, or at least made more predictable, by protecting particularly absorbent materials before and during their service life.

Since high moisture contents can influence bond as well as movements of sealed joints, it may, as with surface temperature, be appropriate to consider defining limits on installation moisture content at the specification stage for some materials.

3.4.3   Irreversible inherent deviations

Irreversible inherent deviations (Sections 1.5, 3.3.3 and 3.3.4.) relate to the inherent material properties and structural behaviour that create a permanent change in joint dimensions. These could include:

- drying shrinkage
- creep
- differential settlement (e.g., between tall/low buildings)
- effects of mining subsidence
- heave.

Such aspects cannot be covered in detail here and will be relevant to different extents for different materials.

Concrete blockwork is particularly susceptible to drying shrinkage, as are calcium silicate bricks. Fired-clay units such as bricks exhibit small reversible movements due to changes in moisture content, but there may also be a permanent and significant moisture expansion in the longer term.

Taking precast concrete as an example, a number of volume changes take place ranging from plastic settlement, plastic shrinkage, early drying shrinkage and early thermal contraction through to long-term drying shrinkage at later stages.

The latter is of considerable concern to a joint designer of precast concrete units, as it will take place after units are brought to site and will continue over extended periods. The extent to which it affects a given unit will be influenced by:

- section shape and size
- concrete mix
- amount of reinforcement
- climatic conditions.

The effect of creep (deformation due to load applied) may also have to be taken into account in variations of joint size. Movements due to creep tend to be sustained but at a diminishing rate after the first year. Some allowance should, however, be considered (BS8110 for concrete).

Detailed prediction of irreversible inherent deviations is beyond the scope of this guide. Individual 'material' codes (e.g., BS8110, BRE Digest 228, BS5628 Pt 3, etc.) should be consulted for more details.

Once predicted levels have been identified, on-site inspection should be considered prior to sealant installation to ensure expected levels are met.

3.4.4 Induced deviations

Those variations in joint width created by the process of manufacture and construction are known as induced deviations. Assessment of likely deviations can be carried out on the basis of measurement; BS5606 was drawn up following compilation of detailed measurements of buildings under construction and provides a detailed reference point for prediction of induced deviations.

Characteristic tolerances (from site measurement) and permissible deviations (i.e., acceptable limits for induced deviations) for various components elements and materials are shown on Tables 3.7, 3.8, 3.9 and 3.10.

It should be noted, however, that in many cases (e.g., brickwork) measurements of characteristic tolerances from BS5606 have been carried out on low-quality structures, so in many cases better tolerances may be achievable. Taking windows in domestic housing as an example, a tolerance of ±20 mm on the opening could result in significant gaps between frame and opening. Good site practice may well recognise such critical dimensions and by using the frame as a 'template' during construction, improved tolerances could be achieved. The precise level should be realistic allowing for current construction methods and is a matter for engineering judgement.

Once permissible deviations have been identified, some estimation of acceptable joint clearance is required. This is outlined in some depth in ISO3443 and *Graphical aid for tolerance and fits* from BRE (R B Bonshor and L L Eldridge, 1974). Induced deviations may, of course, create deviations in all three dimensions of a joint. While a design can take account of these deviations to some extent, if the size of a joint is outside the specified limits, some action is required. This could involve:

- adjusting the position of components to distribute any excess deviations evenly

- special action to correct, for example, tapering of joint clearances, bow and twist of components, inaccurate alignment, etc.
- rejection, as the joint is outside realistic (it is hoped!) specification limits.

Where it is not possible to rectify joints consistently by these means, an alternative joint design may have to be adopted.

Table 3.7 *Permissible deviations of windows*

Frame material	Standard	Length/width	Diagonal	Bow
Wood	BS644: 1989	± 2 mm	3, 5 or 10 mm	3 or 5 mm
Steel	BS6510: 1984	± 1.5 mm	4 mm	-
Aluminium	BS4873: 1986	± 1.5 mm	4 mm	-
PVC-U	BS7412: 1991	± 3 mm	4 mm	-

Table 3.8 *Permissible deviations for curtain walling (Standard for Curtain Walling, CWCT)*

	In any one storey	Overall
Line	± 2 mm	± 5 mm
Level	± 2 mm	± 5 mm
Plumb	± 2 mm	± 5 mm
Plane	± 2 mm	± 5 mm

Table 3.9 *Characteristic building tolerances (BS5606: 1990)*

Material	Window opening	Between walls up to 7m	Between columns	Floor level
Brickwork	± 20 mm	± 20 mm	-	-
Blockwork	-	± 21 mm	-	-
In-situ concrete	± 20 mm	± 24 mm	± 18 mm	± 22 mm
Precast concrete	± 10 mm	± 18 mm	± 13 mm	± 23 mm
Steel	-	-	± 12 mm	± 20 mm

Note: These are tolerances measured on site; in practice about 1 in 20 will be outside these figures.

Table 3.10 *Permissible deviations of non-loadbearing precast concrete cladding (BS8297: 1995)*

		Tolerance values in millimetres
Length and height	Up to 3 m	± 3 mm
	3 m to 6 m	± 5 mm
	6 m to 9 m	± 8 mm
	9 m to 12 m	± 10 mm
Thickness	Up to 500 mm	± 3 mm
	500 mm to 750 mm	± 5 mm
Straightness or bow (deviation from intended line)	Up to 3 m	6 mm
	3 m to 6 m	9 mm
	6 m to 12 m	12 mm
Squareness	Difference in length of two diagonals	3 mm per 2 m of diagonal up to a maximum of 9 mm
Twist	Any corner should not be more than the dimension stated from the plane containing the other three corners.	
Length of longer side	Up to 3 m	6 mm
	3 m to 6 m	9 mm
	6 m to 12 m	12 mm
Openings within one unit (size)		± 6 mm
Openings within one unit (location)	With structural or cover implications	± 6 mm
	Without structural or cover implications	± 12 mm
Anchors and inserts		± 10 mm

Note: The deviations given in Table 3.10 are those that are commonly worked to and have been found to be practicable. They are mostly to finer dimensions than those published in BS8110 as it is felt that for architectural purposes cladding should be made more accurately than structural concrete generally. Attention is drawn to the fact that such accuracy of manufacture is achieved at a higher cost and that improvement on the following dimensions will further materially increase the cost of units and may not be practicable.

3.4.5   Statistical treatment of deviations

When combining separate induced deviations (Section 3.4.4 and Tables 3.7–3.9), the overall induced deviation is calculated from:

$$Y = \pm(d_1{}^2 + d_2{}^2 + d_3{}^2 \ldots)^{0.5}$$

i.e., the overall induced deviation equals the square root of the sum of the squares of individual induced deviations. Hence, where one component has a permissible deviation of ± 3 mm and another a permissible deviation of ± 4 mm, then the total deviation is taken as $\pm (3^2 + 4^2)^{0.5} = 5$ mm. Taking the total deviation as ±7 mm (3 + 4 mm) would be too pessimistic, as it assumes the worst-case deviation in every case.

When considering the overall allowance for deviations in a joint, it may also be appropriate to make allowance for any deviations in the notional size of the space, 'S'.

Hence $\quad Y = \pm (d_1{}^2 + d_2{}^2 + d_3{}^2 \ldots + S^2)^{0.5}$

Because Y is expressed as a ± value, a total variability of 2Y will have to be accommodated over the total building length by (say) n joints. In other words, a range of 2Y/n must be accommodated on each joint, i.e., each the width of each joint will vary between w - Y/n and w + Y/n.

Following the approach outlined in BS5606, for (say) six window frames, each of length 797 mm fitted into a prepared opening, target size 4860 mm, in an in-situ concrete frame:

Number of joints = 7

Variability in space between columns for in-situ concrete
= ± 18 mm (from BS5606, Table 1, T.1.1)

Variability in length of timber windows
= ± 4 mm (from BS5606, Table 2, T.2.1)

Total variability in size of joint, Y
$$= \pm (18^2 + 4^2 + 4^2 + 4^2 + 4^2 + 4^2 + 4^2)^{0.5}$$

$$= \pm 20.5 \text{ mm}$$

Target size of joints $= \dfrac{4860 - (6 \times 797)}{7} = 11.1$ mm each

Maximum joint size $= 11.1 + \dfrac{20.5}{7} = 14$ mm

Minimum joint size $= 11.1 - \dfrac{20.5}{7} = 8.2$ mm

Hence the jointing technique in this case should be capable of accommodating changes due to induced deviations in the range 8.2 to 14 mm. 8.2 mm would then act as the minimum joint width for the purposes of joint design using the 'movement accommodation factor' (Section 3.5). A similar calculation would then be required to assess vertical dimensions.

Inherent deviations must also be accommodated for individual materials in each case. These must be calculated (Section 3.5.1).

Any joint design must allow realistic variations to be incorporated into the structure using available resources. If this proves difficult, a less 'demanding' joint could be considered. In the extreme, the most tolerant option of open joints with supporting gasket seals may become the most realistic option.

In summary, the concept of tolerances is essentially linked with the idea of buildability and needs to be realistically addressed throughout the building process. Key stages for the joint designer include:

- design
  - use less 'demanding' details if possible
  - justify 'demanding' details
  - determine required accuracy
  - define permissible deviations
  - highlight crucial areas

- documentation - define tolerances

- construction
  - monitor
  - consider suggestion/alternative proposals
  - consider options for out of tolerance areas

Procedures for dealing with characteristic accuracies in buildings are outlined in depth in BS5606 and BS6954: Pt 3. BS5606 also outlines further examples of tolerance in buildings, while predicted effects of inaccuracies on joint widths are detailed in BRE Digest 199.

3.5 DESIGN PROCEDURES

Previous sections have outlined the supporting concept of why a joint is required (Section 1), what material to use (Section 2), what movements must be taken into account (Sections 1 and 3), and what deviations must be considered (Section 3.4). By this stage, the designer should also have given appropriate consideration to the adjacent substrate materials, both in terms of behaviour in service (Section 1) and adhesion characteristics (Sections 2.5.5 and 2.7.3). The aim of this section is to review the basic procedures of sealed butt joint design. The same principles could be applied to lap joints, provided the specifier is satisfied that the joint can be installed and maintained correctly. The use of fillet joints to accommodate movement is generally not recommended; if used, they should be designed as outlined in Section 3.2.1.

3.5.1 Joint design

The calculation of appropriate joint width for a wet-applied sealant in a joint subject to movement is given by:

$$W = \frac{M \times 100}{MAF} + M + Y$$

where:
W	=	design joint width	- Section 3.5.2
M	=	total expected movement (due to inherent deviations)	- Section 3.3
MAF	=	movement accommodation factor	- Section 3.5.2
Y	=	overall induced deviation	- Section 3.4.5

The derivation of this equation and a worked example is given in Section 3.5.2.

Having calculated the appropriate joint width (and checked that the figure is acceptable) an appropriate depth for the sealant type and movement should be identified (Section 3.2.1).

3.5.2 Joint design equation

The movement accommodation factor (MAF) of a sealant can be defined as the total movement that a sealant is capable of tolerating, expressed as a percentage of theoretical minimum butt joint width (Section 2.8.1). It is expressed as a total change in joint dimension from minimum to maximum, not a ± movement.

Hence $MAF(\%) = \frac{M \times 100}{W_1}$

i.e., total estimated movement range, $M = MAF/100 \times W_1$

where MAF   =   movement accommodation factor
       W_1 =   theoretical minimum joint width
or W_1 =   (M × 100)/MAF

For example, if MAF = 25%, M = 5 mm, then

W_1 =   (5 × 100)/25

         =   20 mm

Hence a sealant of low MAF (e.g., oil-based mastic) can accommodate only a small movement after sealing (approximately 10% of initial joint width). Conversely, a high MAF sealant (e.g., silicone) can accommodate far greater movement without failure (25 to 50% of joint width).

The total allowable movement range is, therefore, directly proportional both to the flexibility of the sealant (as defined by MAF) and the assumed theorectical minimum joint width at the time of sealing. If the joint is smaller than specified at the time of sealing, the allowable movement range will inevitably be reduced. Such changes could result from inherent or induced deviations (Section 3.4).

In particular the installation temperature, if outside the specified range, can ruin the validity of the joint width calculations due to creation of (for example) too narrow a joint.

Inherent deviations

If a joint is sealed when thermal expansion or other inherent deviation have given rise to a reduction in the size of a joint, subsequent cooling and resultant widening of the joint will create an increased strain on the installed sealant. This necessitates the calculation of a larger joint width, W_2, to allow for those deviations. If, however, it is assumed that a joint is sealed when at its narrowest (i.e., when the joint width is W_1-M) the flexibility of the sealant will be related directly to the maximum strain it should encounter throughout its life.

Hence estimated total movement range, M = MAF/100 × (W_2 - M)

Or   M × 100/MAF = (W_2 - M)

Or W_2 = (M × 100)/MAF + M   ...[1]

For example, if MAF = 25%, M = 5 mm, then

W_2 = (5 × 100)/25 + 5

         = 25 mm

This makes some allowance for inherent variations in joint width when sealing. The equation makes allowance for construction during coldest weather (creating wide joints) followed by sealing during hottest (which creates potential for maximum stress on the sealant). The joint width obtained provides a guide for the minimum width permissible at the time of sealing, and also defines the appropriate depth of sealant that should be applied to the joint (Section 2.8). Installing a narrower width of sealant could lead to a greater risk of failure.

Induced deviations

While expected movements in joints are addressed through the above equation, joints also have to allow for induced deviations (Section 3.4). Failure to allow for such deviations could again result in, for example, a sealed joint being narrower than expected, with the predicted movements potentially forming a higher than expected percentage of initial joint width. The MAF of the sealant may then be exceeded and failure is likely.

Hence Equation 1 above must be modified to take account of induced deviations such as inaccuracies in manufacture, placing of components, etc. This will again lead to an increased joint width, W.

The designer must, therefore:

- estimate permissible deviations (induced) at the joint
- specify a joint width that allows for them (i.e., assumes as a worst case that the joint is sealed when at its narrowest).

Hence $W \quad = \quad W_2 + Y$

Where Y is the permissable induced deviation,

$$Y = (d_1^2 + d_2^2 + d_3^2 + S^2)^{0.5}$$

and W = design joint width (since all deviations have now been taken into account).

Joint design process

Key stages in the design of sealed joints, therefore, are:

- calculation of M, expected movements
- selection of sealant of given flexibility (MAF)
- calculation (including allowance for deviations) of joint width
- check: is joint width acceptable?

If, after calculating the joint width by these means, the result is unacceptable, it will be necessary to consider:

- reassessment of movements/deviations to ensure they are realistic
- use of sealant of different MAF
- more frequent joints
- different, more accommodating joint system (e.g., use of lap joints if they can be installed correctly – Section 3.2.1).

This 'loop' will be visited many times in most joint designs until the correct balance of material and joint type is obtained. Once the correct sealant width has been established, an appropriate width:depth ratio must be selected before specification (Section 3.2.1).

This process is summarised on the flowchart, Figure 3.6.

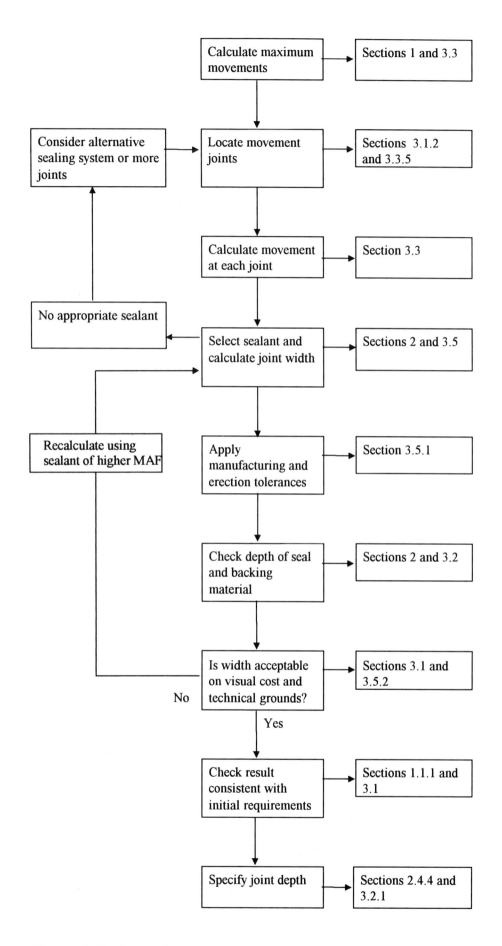

Figure 3.6 *The joint design process*

Example: Calculation of joint width for a vertical butt joint

a) Calculation of movement

Consider a precast concrete construction, panel length 5 m

Assume temperature range = -20 to + 50°C

Installation temperature = 5 to 40°C (assume 5°C when installed)

Temperature rise (surface) = 45°C

Temperature drop (surface) = 25°C

Bulk temperature resulting from this surface temperature will depend on a number of factors (Section 3.4.2) and will vary considerably from a low-conductivity precast concrete panel to a highly responsive aluminium facade. Similarly, the resultant movement (e.g., linear expansion or bowing) will vary according to both the restraint and thermal gradient experienced by the element.

For this precast concrete element, assume linear movement and that bulk temperature can be taken as the average of the concrete inner and outer surface temperatures. (Note that for a highly conductive and isolated element such as an aluminium panel, the surface temperatures will be practically identical.)

Coefficient of thermal expansion = $12 \times 10^{-6}/°C$

Thermal expansion = $12 \times 10^{-6} \times 5000 \times 45/2 = 1.35$ mm ...[2]

Thermal contraction = $12 \times 10^{-6} \times 5000 \times 25/2 = 0.75$ mm ...[3]

Assume reversible moisture movement = 0.02%

OR 0.01% about mean size = $\dfrac{0.01}{100} \times 5000 = 0.5$ mm ...[4]

Assume irreversible moisture movement = $100 \times 10^{-6} \times 5000 = 0.5$ mm ...[5]

(See BS8110: Part 2, 1985, Figure 7.2 for appropriate figure.)

Total expansion [2] + [4] = 1.35 + 0.5 = 1.85 mm

Total contraction [3] + [4] + [5] = 0.75 + 0.5 + 0.5 = 1.75 mm

Total movement range = 3.6 mm

b) First calculation of joint width

Assuming appropriate (for example, durability, substrate adhesion and environmental) considerations have been taken into account, movement capability of the selected sealant can now be addressed.

From Section 3.5.1 above, assume:

$$\text{Design joint width, } W = \frac{M \times 100}{MAF} + M + Y \qquad ...[6]$$

where

M = total expected movement

MAF = movement accommodation factor

Y = deviations (will vary according to job specifications and materials used; Section 3.4)

Hence for (say) a polysulfide sealant with movement accommodation factor of 25%, we have:

Design joint width $= (3.6 \times 100)/25 + 3.6 + Y$

Assume $Y = 15$ mm

(See BS8110: Part 1, 1997, Clause 5.2.4 for appropriate figure.)

which gives a design joint width $= 14.4 + 3.6 + 15 = 33$mm approximately

Clearly, if a sealant of higher or lower MAF were used, the corresponding joint widths would be reduced or increased respectively. Once the width has been established, selection of an appropriate joint depth for effective performance is essential (Section 3.2.1).

The calculation assumes an even distribution of movement on all joints on the building. In reality, certain joints may lock up and concentrate movements elsewhere. By making certain assumptions (e.g., contribution of support structure to reduce movement) the joint width may be reduced. It is important, however, to ensure that any such reductions are made in a carefully thought out and consistent way.

For simplicity, this example only assumes vertical joints in a precast concrete structure. Differential settlement and/or structural loading are not, therefore, included. Horizontal joints would have to make allowance for such factors (using Table 3.5 and appropriate material codes) and may, therefore, be much wider than this figure.

3.5.3 Design for replacement

Having established the expected life of a sealant (Section 2), if it is less durable than the surrounding elements it is essential to consider the consequences of sealant replacement in the future. The designer may try to balance initial materials costs against long-term maintenance costs. The designer should, therefore:

- design joints that allow safe access for maintenance, inspection and (if required) replacement
- ensure minimal damage to the fabric in the event of repair/replacement
- ensure resealing operations (e.g., joint cleaning) can be carried out with minimal disruption.

All sealants will (eventually) fail; the sealant life will generally be less than the design life of the joint and the building within which it is located.

In terms of specifying sealants for replacement, it may be appropriate to select a sealant whose lifetime corresponds with other scaffolding or maintenance requirements rather than a sealant that may last 10 years longer but requires its own costly replacement programme. Liaison between client/tenant/architect/QS/engineer/contractor in a 'total design' approach could help achievement of such an objective.

The system of water and air seals is also important to consider at this stage. A single-sealant joint creates a single air and water barrier. Such joints will generally be exposed on the outside face of the building, and, as such, create an increased risk of water penetration into the building should the seal fail.

If two sealant joints are used, water and air barriers can be separated. The water barrier remains on the outside as a rainscreen, but is separated by a drained cavity from the internal air barrier. In this way, the joint life can be extended (Section 4.2).

The joint design should allow access for maintenance, inspection and (if required) replacement. At the same time, however, protection/recessing of seals may be useful to extend sealant life. Lap joints for example, while excellent in terms of movement accommodation and 'shielding' from the elements, are difficult (if not impossible) to prime, seal, inspect and maintain (Figure 3.7).

Sealant difficult to inspect
and inaccessible

Sealant accessible for
maintenance

Figure 3.7 *Resealing of lap joints*

Conventional butt and recessed joints can also be designed with accessibility in mind (Figure 3.8).

Limited accessibility

Improved accessibility

Figure 3.8 *Resealing butt joints*

Joints between wall/roof sheets (Figure 3.9) are inaccessible for maintenance, but tend not to need much movement accommodation and are shielded from the elements. The detail is not ideal, but is generally found to provide acceptable performance in warehouse-style structures, for example, provided the sheets are adequately fixed.

Figure 3.9 *Inaccessible joints*

There will always be conflicts that the joint designer has to consider (Section 3.1.1). The designer may consider the relative merits of designing joints, for example, by consideration of accessibility, appearance, durability and health and safety (Sections 3.1.1 and 3.1.5). The individual joint designer must find the correct balance in each case.

3.5.4   Durability within the sealant life cycle

Durability of sealants has already been addressed in Sections 2.9 and 2.10. Durability concerns also raise several issues for design of sealant joints that are addressed here.

Poorly specified low-grade sealants are all too frequently used in onerous applications where their low initial material cost turns into a much higher 'life cycle' cost due to premature failure.

Such 'failure' could be judged as, for example:

- weathering/long-term deterioration
- adhesive/cohesive failure
- surface appearance
- need for maintenance (perhaps linked with replacement of adjacent elements)
- vandalism
- safety (e.g., soft/extractable sealant creating a health hazard).

The next step could range from local replacement of failed sealant or (less ideally) 'capping' with a replacement sealant through to full-scale replacement and resealing (Section 2.11).

Such measures will be required at some stage for most sealant joints in the external envelope of buildings.

Even if a top-quality appropriate and 'durable' sealant is selected and correctly installed, failure of the sealant during the life of the facade is to be expected. In selection of a material for a sealant joint, therefore, one must consider:

1. What is the expected life in relation to the required life of the building?

2. When sealants are to be replaced, are they accessible? Will their location make resealing difficult?

3. What maintenance will be required?

4. What sealant could/should be used for resealing?

A case study was carried out in 1990 that illustrates the criticality of these points in more detail. For a building in the north-west of England, an estimate for sealant works was obtained as follows:

- sealant (@ £4/litre)   3875 litres   £15,500
- installation, cradles, etc.   (30 + weeks work)   £46,500
- total cost   £62,000

At a late stage, however, an alternative proposal was accepted:

- sealant (@ £2/litre)   3875 litres   £7,750
- installation   £23,250
- total cost   £31,000

The second, cheaper proposal (a saving of some £31,000) used an oil-based mastic material, of inferior movement and durability characteristics when compared to the originally proposed polysulfide sealant.

Not surprisingly, the oil-based mastic failed prematurely, in this case due to inadequate movement capability, within two years of installation. The total cost of the supposedly 'cheaper' option became:

- removal and replacement labour   £92,500
- cradles (40 + weeks)   £28,000
- sealant (@ £4/litre)   £15,500
- total extra cost   £136,000

In this example, therefore, an initial 'saving' of £31,000 became an ultimate total cost of £167,000, some £105,000 more expensive than the original estimate. In addition, this figure does not document those undisclosed costs in terms of, for example, legal fees, disruption and potential loss of client confidence in materials, manufacturer, specifier and contractor.

While these costs will undoubtedly vary from region to region and from year to year, the implications for materials selection are clear: be aware of total 'life cycle' cost (including, for example, costs of materials/labour/access and discounted renewal/maintenance costs). It is not just materials costs that should be considered when specifying sealants.

For more information on resealing see *Resealing of Buildings – a Guide to Good Practice*, by R Woolman and A Hutchinson, 1994.

3.6   SPECIFIER'S CHECK-LIST

By working through Sections 1, 2 and 3 of this guide, the various procedures required for successful sealant selection are carried out. By this stage, the designer should have considered all stages with the exception of installation (Section 5) and may already have provisionally selected a sealant material on durability and/or other performance grounds. A 'check-list' of key considerations that should be covered in the specification is given below. See also Figure 1, Decision-making process for design of a sealant joint, in the Introduction.

Property	Specification requirement (fill in for each case as appropriate)	Source of information
Overall considerations (e.g., CDM, environment)	— — — — — — — — — — — — —	Section 3.1
Sources of movement	— — — — — — — — — — — — —	Sections 1.6 and 3.3
Magnitude of movement	— — — — — — — — — — — — —	Sections 3.3 and 1.6
Temperature range - for installation	— — — — — — — — — — — —	Sections 1.6.1 and 3.3.2
- in service	— — — — — — — — — — — —	
Ease of replacement	— — — — — — — — — — —	Sections 2.11.2 and 3.5.4
Cost	— — — — — — — — — — —	Section 3.5.3
Substrate materials	— — — — — — — — — — —	Sections 1.3, 2.7.3 and 4
Deviations	— — — — — — — — — — —	Section 3.4
Sealant material	— — — — — — — — — — —	Sections 2 and 3.1.1
Joint design (joint width)	— — — — — — — — — — —	Sections 2.4.3, 3.5.1 and 3.5.2
Joint shape (width:depth ratio)	— — — — — — — — — — —	Sections 2.8 and 3.2.1
Bond breaker/backer	— — — — — — — — — — —	Sections 2.3.2 and 3.2.2
Installation	— — — — — — — — — — —	Section 5
Site records	— — — — — — — — — — —	Section 5

Various approaches to sealant selection and specification exist. Provided adequate consideration (in combination with material suppliers) is given to the above factors, the task of successful materials selection and specification is considerably simplified.

4   Construction details

This section gives guidance on the detailed construction of sealant joints within the building envelope. Emphasis is placed on the location and type of joints to be used, and the role of sealant joints in multi-layer walls. Section 2 provides full details of the sealant system selection process. Section 3 gives guidance on the design of sealant joints to accommodate movement and tolerances.

4.1   GENERAL

The construction details illustrated have been selected to demonstrate the principles of joint design. The examples are not exhaustive. The designer should use these examples to inform the particular design, not copy them exactly. They show sealing of:

- wall joints in brickwork or blockwork
- precast or poured in-situ concrete panels
- mechanically fixed stone panels
- metal wall and roof panels
- rainscreen walls
- windows into walls
- window assemblies
- wall penetrations
- roof penetrations
- parapets
- curtain wall interfaces
- slope glazing interfaces.

The drawings are not dimensioned: all sealant joints should be of sufficient width and depth to accommodate movements and tolerances calculated as shown in Section 3.

4.2   MULTI-LAYERED SEALING SYSTEMS

The building envelope is too often considered as a two-dimensional plane surface with joints to be sealed. In general, the building envelope is a more complex structure, requiring an appropriate system of joints and seals. A single skin joined with a single joint rarely occurs (probably only for metal skins with no insulation or inner lining). In reality, most walls have an inside and an outside that are joined, and sealed, separately.

4.2.1   Secondary defence systems

Increasingly, walls are being constructed with inner and outer layers and large intermediate cavities. These may be the extensive cavities between a rainscreen and a back-up wall or a cavity left between a window frame and wall (Figure 4.17). For walls containing cavities, it is essential to permit ventilation of the cavity and drainage from the cavity. This is even the case for cavity brick walls for which weep holes are provided near to the base of the cavity.

Figures 4.5, 4.8, 4.23, and 4.25 show details of weep tubes and drainage openings in different wall constructions. These pass through the sealant joint (including the backer rod) or bypass the joint to drain water from the cavity to the outer surface. Similar details should be incorporated in other seals where appropriate, for instance to drain the cavity created between a window sub-sill and a wall, Figure 4.22. When considering layered envelope construction with more than one line of defence, it is useful to separate the functions of water sealing and air sealing.

Water seals

Water sealing may be achieved by:

- open joints
- baffled joints
- gaskets
- wet-applied sealants
- sealant tape
- cellular sealing strips.

Air seals

Air sealing may be achieved by:

- gaskets
- wet-applied sealants
- sealant tapes
- cellular sealing strips.

This guide is concerned primarily with the use of wet-applied sealants and cellular sealing strips. Where two lines of defence are used these may be used as the seal in either, or both, joints. Designers should also consider the use of open labyrinthine joints, baffled joints and gaskets.

4.2.2   Primary defence systems

It may happen that the functions of water sealing and air sealing are both satisfied by a primary, single seal – for instance joints in a single-layer sheet-metal roof sealed with wet-applied sealant or a sealant tape (Sections 4.11 and 4.12).

Primary defence systems are inherently less robust than secondary defence systems. Failure of a single seal will allow air leakage through the wall. The air movements and pressure difference across the joint will then drive water past the seal. For a similar failure of the outer seal in a secondary defence system, less water will leak past the outer seal, and will be able to drain out of the wall.

With a single line of defence there is also a conflict between the need to create an air seal and the desire to provide weep tubes to remove inadvertent leakage water. It is seldom possible to drain water from behind a single line of defence and achieve acceptable low air leakage through the wall. All too often water leaks past the single line of defence and is retained within the fabric of the building envelope.

4.2.3   Joint configuration

Joints are arranged to accommodate movement and tolerance, to incorporate separate, or combined, water and air seals, match the geometry and positions of the components, be buildable and maintainable.

Accommodation of tolerance

The tolerances of components and gaps are described and calculated in Section 3.4. Tolerances may be accommodated by, for instance, taking a butt joint of sufficient width as calculated in Section 3.5 to allow for in-plane tolerances. Alternatively, the components to be joined can be overlapped to allow for tolerance and a lap joint used to make the seal. The sealant in this joint does not have to be sized to accommodate tolerance as allowance is made in the geometry of the gap.

This aspect of allowing for tolerances can be illustrated with the installation of windows, which may be butted to the adjacent wall (Figure 4.17) or lapped behind the outer leaf of the wall (Figure 4.19). In the latter case, the size of the sealant joint does not have to consider accommodation of in-plane deviation. Of course, any out-of-plane deviation must still be accommodated, but this is often smaller than in-plane deviation.

Exposed joints

Some of the details presented show the use of sealant systems in an exposed position. Joints that are exposed are readily accessible for inspection and resealing. However, sealant materials used in this way are exposed to UV, temperature change, atmosphere and rain to a great extent and will age faster (Section 2.9). A higher-performance sealant may be required to provide the desired sealant service life in these situations. Alternatively, a shorter service life and resealing may be accepted.

Concealed joints

Some of the sealant joints shown in the details are, from necessity, concealed within the structure of the wall and therefore not accessible for inspection and maintenance. Sealant materials used in these joints cannot easily be replaced during the service life of the wall and so must be selected to give the optimum service life. However, sealant materials in concealed joints will, to some extent, be in a moderated climate that extends their service life (by, for instance, not being exposed to UV or extremes of temperature). Many such concealed joints are air seals and the demands made of them are less than those required of water seals. Different materials, such as cellular sealing strips, may be used and very different selection criteria may then apply to the materials.

4.3 JOINT DRAWINGS

Joints have to be designed, detailed and dimensioned. They should also be drawn. In particular, drawings of joints at the interfaces between separate subcontracts or packages of work should be available. Responsibility for production, co-ordination and updating of these drawings should be decided at an early stage once the joint designer has been appointed (Section 1.2.1).

Many component suppliers now make drawings of their products available in CAD format. A designer can import a drawing of a window, and even the sealant joints associated with it, into a drawing of a wall with little thought for how the window-to-wall joint works, how the head/jamb and jamb/sill intersections are detailed or how the seals correlate to the flashings, damp-proof membranes and drainage paths. This ability to draw on CAD systems without thinking through the function and detailed design of the joint has increased the need for checking or auditing of the details at interfaces.

Drawings showing joint details at interfaces should be available to both subcontractors and main contractors and there should be a procedure for commenting on and amending details. Drawings should be drawn large-scale and fully dimensioned showing tolerances. They should show substrates, flashings, dpms and materials of the sealant system.

4.4 TYPICAL JOINT DETAILS

The appropriate detailing of a joint will depend on both of the components to be joined. For a multi-layered wall it will also require the correct co-ordination of the two components to be joined.

The number of combinations of components and different geometries is very large. The joint details in this section have been selected to demonstrate principles of joint construction and to present a number of typical good practice solutions. Tables 4.1 and 4.2 show the figure numbers of the details that are appropriate, or may be modified, to create particular joints.

Table 4.1 *Joint details appropriate for different cladding materials*

Cladding materials	Panel to panel horizontal	Panel to panel vertical	To structural frame	Windows and doors	Penetrations
Concrete panels	4.4 4.5	4.1 4.2 4.3	4.6	4.28 4.29 4.30	(4.40)
Dimensioned stone	4.9	(4.9)	–	(4.31) (4.32) (4.33)	(4.40)
Brickwork	4.7, 4.8	4.9	–	4.17–4.24	4.40
Metal over-cladding	4.13, 4.14	4.13, 4.14	–	4.31 4.32 4.33	(4.40) (4.41)
Profiled metal	4.12	4.11	–	4.25 4.26 4.27	(4.40) (4.41)
GFRP/GRC	(4.13) (4.14)	(4.13) (4.14)	–	(4.31) (4.32) (4.33)	–
Masonry inner leaf			4.10	4.10	

Note: Figure 4.10 identifies water and air seal position for a clad wall with a masonry back

( ) denotes details that may be applicable

Table 4.2 *Joint details appropriate for different building components*

Components	Cavity wall	Rainscreen wall	Glazing systems	Profiled metal	Heavyweight cladding
Window/door head	4.23	4.31	–	4.25	4.28
Window/door jamb	4.17–4.20	4.32	–	4.26	(4.28)
Window/door sill	4.21 4.22 4.24	4.33	–	4.27	4.29
Connecting mullions	–	–	4.16	–	–
Curtain wall perimeter	4.34 4.35 4.36	–	–	–	4.34 (4.35) (4.36)
Penetrations	4.40	(4.40)	–	4.41	(4.40)
Parapets	–	4.39	–	4.39	–
Slope glazing	4.38 4.37	–	–	–	4.38 4.37

Note: Figure 4.15 is a key reference drawing for Figures 4.16–4.30, showing frame and fixing details.

4.4.1   Concrete walls

Concrete walls may be constructed as poured in-situ concrete or precast panels. The movements to be accommodated will depend on the form of wall construction, type of supporting structure and method of attachment to the structure.

Concrete walls may be sealed using drained joints or joints dependent on a primary seal, (Figures 4.1–4.6). Joints that rely on a single face seal are more likely to fail as they are in an exposed position, and the consequences of failure are invariably water ingress into the fabric of the building. For this reason joints containing a secondary inner seal are to be preferred.

Water may leak through the concrete and bypass an outer seal. The back-up of the outer seal must be tolerant of moisture. The sealant used in the outer seal must adhere to the substrate when it is wetted from behind.

Inner air seals may be breached by a structural element passing through the wall or built into the inner face of the wall, Figure 4.6.

Joints are often recessed to reduce visual impact. This may also make it easier to prime and seal (Section 3.2.1).

Some silicones, polyurethanes and one-part polysulfides may stain concrete (Section 2.9)

Poured in-situ concrete

In-situ concrete will undergo initial moisture movement due to drying shrinkage (Section 1.6.2). However, thermal movement is small due to the high thermal mass of the concrete. Structural movements due to loading (Section 1.6.3) will be of limited extent due to the rigidity of the structure. Spacing of the joints will depend primarily on the need to prevent shrinkage cracking (Section 3.3.5).

Precast concrete

Some of the initial shrinkage of the panels will occur before they are attached to the building, but shrinkage continues for several months after casting. With the exception of some lightweight panels such as GRC, thermal movement is also limited.

Movement of the panels relative to one another will depend on the stiffness of the structural frame and the method of attachment (Section 1.4). Out-of-plane movements arising from wind loading, and thermal and moisture movement are controlled by the position of the fixings and the degree of restraint they provide. Tolerances are a major consideration when designing the joints between precast concrete panels and induced deviations have to be calculated when determining the width and spacing of joints (Section 3.4).

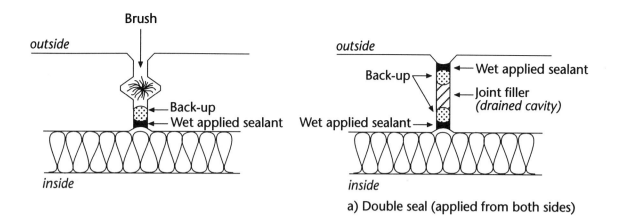

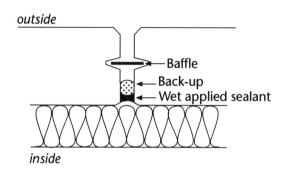

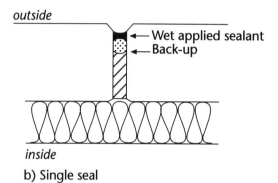

a) Double seal (applied from both sides)

b) Single seal

Figure 4.1 *Precast concrete panels (vertical baffled joints)*

These joints are commonly referred to as drained joints.

The inner seal provides the air seal in the wall and may be constructed as a butt joint using a wet-applied sealant or a cellular sealing strip.

The primary defence against water ingress is the baffle, either of strip or brush form. The inner seal is in a protected position but the drained cavity is not a totally dry environment. If the joint is made from the inside as shown, the back-up for the sealant should be tolerant of occasional wetting during driving rain.

Figure 4.2 *Concrete panels (vertical face-sealed joints)*

For both precast and in-situ concrete walls it is possible to face-seal joints. For in-situ concrete a filler board is likely to be left in the joint as a joint filler. For precast panels this may be present to allow secure placement of the back-up and subsequently the sealant.

In porous substrates water may bypass the face seal and enter the cavity or filler. If this is a possibility, consideration should be given to the use of a double sealed joint as shown in Figure 4.3.

An inner seal may also be provided to protect the compressible joint filler or create a secondary air seal. The joint then behaves as a secondary defence system and the cavity must be drained.

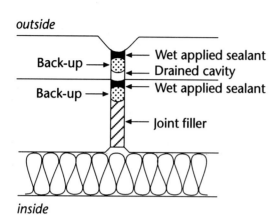

outside

Back-up → Wet applied sealant

— Drained cavity

Back-up → Wet applied sealant

— Joint filler

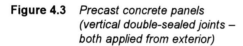

inside

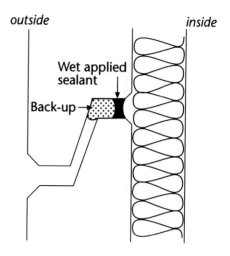

outside   inside

Wet applied sealant

Back-up →

Figure 4.3 *Precast concrete panels (vertical double-sealed joints – both applied from exterior)*

Precast concrete panels may be constructed with a dense concrete structural panel faced with a more porous layer of reconstituted stone or brickwork. Face-sealed joints in these panels may fail due to water seeping through the porous layer and bypassing the seal. If this is likely to occur then either a double-sided sealed joint (Figure 4.2) should be used or a second seal should be made set back from the outer face and bridging between the less permeable concrete inner substrates.

The primary seal against water ingress is the outer seal. However, water will enter the cavity between the two seals, which should be drained at its base. The outer seal will not provide an air seal as a result of the drainage paths through it and the only air seal is the inner seal.

The inner seal is protected from UV light and weather but is still in a moist environment. The sealant system may not be the same as that in the outer seal.

It may be necessary to construct a joint of this form if access to the back of the joint is restricted. However, it may be difficult to apply the sealant to make the inner seal. Consideration should be given to the use of cellular sealing strips to make the inner seal.

Figure 4.4 *Precast concrete panels (horizontal single-sealed joints)*

This joint performs in a similar manner to a vertical baffled joint. However, a baffle is not required and any water entering the joint drains to the outer face.

If the sealant joint is placed at the outer face (for ease of construction) then water passing the seal does not immediately flow to the inner face if the gap is sloped as shown. Water seeping into the joint from the upper panel will be returned in the joint by the seal at the outer face. It may then seep from the joint into the lower panel before it overflows to the inner face of the wall. However, single-line-of-defence face seals are inherently less robust than the inner seal and drained joint shown.

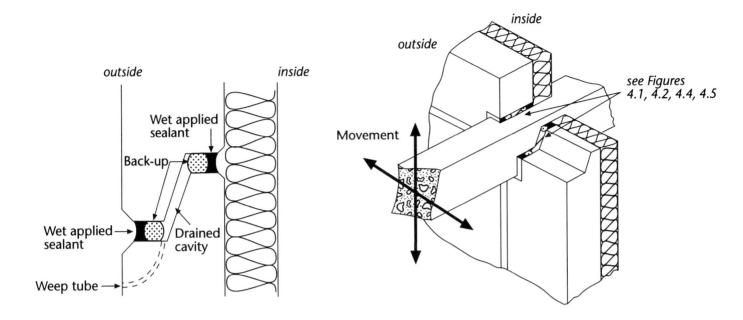

Figure 4.5 *Precast concrete panels (horizontal double-sealed joint)*

This joint performs in a similar way to a vertical double-sealed joint. However, water entering the cavity between the two seals will not drain along the joint and must be drained to the outer face of the wall. This is best achieved by the provision of weep tubes or weep holes.

Sloping the joint gap as shown so that the inner seal is above the outer seal will ensure that water drains away from the inner seal.

Some precast walls are designed with elaborate internal drainage systems to carry water from the joint cavities. Water is either drained from the head of a panel to its foot or into rainwater pipes incorporated in the wall.

Figure 4.6 *Precast concrete panels (sealing to a structural frame)*

Where a structural framing member completely penetrates a precast concrete wall it is necessary to create a weather seal between the two. If a structural frame penetrates the inner air barrier of a wall then the inner air seals should be sealed against the framing member.

Such a joint is likely to be made at the intersection of several panels and has to accommodate movement of the panels relative to each other and to the frame.

Movement of these joints can be minimised by attaching the panels at fixing positions close to the joint.

For double-sealed joints with drained cavities and for open-drained joints, water falling in the vertical cavity above the penetration will have to be diverted around the framing member. It should not drain towards the inner face of the wall. Careful consideration has to be given to the use of internal flashings and seals to ensure a good weather seal and internal drainage paths around this intersection.

4.4.2   Brickwork and blockwork walls

Brick and blockwork may be used in loadbearing walls and in non-loadbearing form as a brick outer skin on a structural frame. Most bricks and blocks are permeable to water and the mortar joints are yet more permeable. Water will pass through a single skin of brick or blockwork and a cavity has to be provided to intercept and drain away this leakage water.

Water will often bypass a single seal in the outer face of a wall. Seals are provided to prevent gross water leakage at a joint. The back-up of the outer seal must be tolerant of moisture and the sealant used in the outer seal must adhere to the substrate when it is wetted from behind.

As the cavity in the wall is drained and ventilated the inner leaf of a wall should be constructed to act as an air barrier. It should be sealed to the air barrier of adjacent elements, components and penetrations such as floor slabs and structural frames (Figure 4.8).

Some silicones, polyurethanes and one-part polysulfides may stain bricks, blocks or mortar (Section 2.9).

Non-loadbearing walls

Non-loadbearing brickwork or blockwork is constructed as panels to co-ordinate with the structural frame of the building. Joints have to accommodate both structural movement and expansion/contraction of the bricks or blocks. The magnitude of structural movements will depend on the form of construction of the structural frame. Joint spacing in non-loadbearing brickwork is often governed by the position of structural frame members. Out-of-plane movements due to wind loading depend on the position of restraints and their effectiveness.

Loadbearing walls

Vertical joints are provided to accommodate expansion and contraction of the brickwork (Figure 4.7). Joint spacing is governed by the type of bricks or blocks to be used and should be calculated (Section 3.3.5).

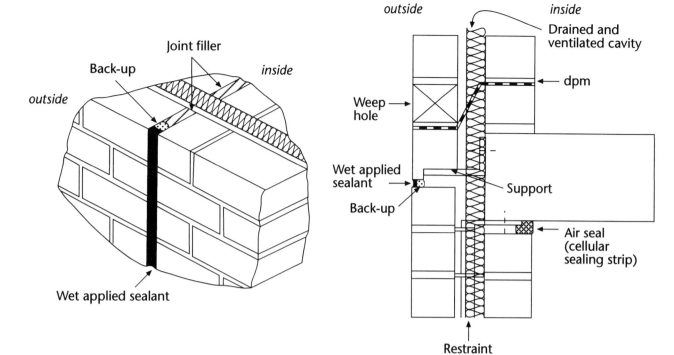

Figure 4.7   *Brickwork (vertical joint)*

A compressible filler is often incorporated in the joint to facilitate bricklaying and gauge the width of the joint. However, the faces of the joint are unlikely to be plane – some bricks may be set back or forward from the joint; similarly for the mortar joints. Any abrupt change in joint width will act as a stress raiser in the sealant and is a potential failure point in the sealant joint.

Attention to accurate bricklaying at the joint face will lead to a better seal performance and reduce the risk of premature failure.

Figure 4.8   *Brickwork (horizontal joint)*

Horizontal sealed joints are provided to accommodate vertical building movement and movement of the brickwork panel. They are generally provided at each storey height. The upper panel of brickwork is supported on a loadbearing bracket. The lower panel should be restrained against wind loading.

Similar attention to accurate bricklaying applies as for a vertical sealed joint. However, the joint filler does not serve to form an accurate joint gap and may be omitted. Greater care will be required to position the back-up correctly. The advantage of omitting the filler is that water bypassing the seal can drain freely into a drained cavity between the inner and outer leafs.

4.4.3 Dimensioned stone

Dimensioned stone is constructed as separate units mechanically fixed to an inner blockwork wall or fixed to a support frame as part of a panellised/unitised curtain wall. Individual units may be larger than 600 mm × 900 mm. Moisture movement and thermal movement will depend on the type of stone and method of fixing. This movement is accommodated locally by the joint around each individual stone unit. Most dimensioned stone used in the UK is 40 mm or more thick and has a high thermal mass. However, some proprietary systems use stone bonded onto a reinforced resin or aluminium panel. These thinner stone units (10–20 mm) experience greater thermal movements and moisture movements and are not commonly used on buildings in the UK. The magnitude of any structural movements will depend on the form of the structural frame and loadings on it. The structural movement may be distributed across many joints that typically are 15–20 mm wide or concentrated at joints that coincide with movement joints in the structural support wall. The width of all joints should be calculated (Section 3.5.2).

Dimensioned stone may be constructed with open joints or sealed with a single face seal (Figure 4.9). Water leakage through or around the seal is drained back into a cavity. A drained cavity is essential to deal with any inadvertent leakage and water seeping through the stone outer leaf. An effective air barrier is required behind the ventilated cavity. The air barrier may be either a masonry inner leaf (Figure 4.10) or, in the case of a panellised curtain wall, it may be a metal inner skin (Figure 4.14). In both cases the air barrier should be continuous, sealed to all penetrations and to the air barriers of adjacent components.

Some silicones, polyurethanes and one-part polysulfides may stain stone (Section 2.9).

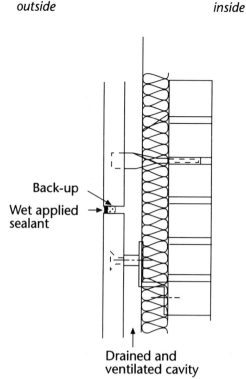

Figure 4.9 *Dimensioned stone*

Dimensioned stone is normally supplied with square-cut edges such that horizontal joints cannot be sloped to promote drainage. For this reason a single face seal and a drained cavity are required to drain away any inadvertent leakage.

Ideally, the stones should each have a V cut into the edge to provide a well-defined location for the back-up. However, much stone has plane square-cut edges, and the back-up must then be placed with care and gauged for depth. It is important not to disturb the back-up during sealant application.

The sealing of thin stone units (40 mm) may be difficult if they are fixed by their edges using kerfs or dowels. Back fixing with undercut anchors may allow use of a deeper sealant section, a better back-up or construction of a recessed joint.

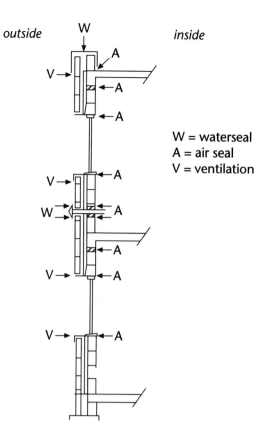

W = waterseal
A = air seal
V = ventilation

Figure 4.10 *Masonry back walls*

Dimensioned stone, metal panels, GFRP, GRC and similar cladding systems are often attached to a brick or blockwork infill panel or spandrel wall. This inner wall forms the air barrier behind a ventilated cavity and should be sealed accordingly.

Masonry walls used to form an air barrier should be sealed at all windows/doors and penetrations and should be sealed to all adjacent wall elements such as curtain walling. Infill panels should be detailed to prevent gross air leakage between the panel and surrounding frame.

Internal finishes such as plasters and some paints provide a good air seal. Dry lining systems can seldom be sealed effectively at their head, foot or penetrations for plumbing and wiring. Some air leakage is acceptable, but an air barrier should be identified in every wall and should be made continuous to limit the flow of air into the building. Gross air leakage will cause excessive heat loss.

4.4.4 Metal cladding

Metal cladding is incorporated into building envelopes in the following forms:

- profiled metal (as a single- or double-skin construction)
- profiled or flat sheets as a composite insulated panel
- metal panels acting as a rainscreen
- metal panels used as infill panels in curtain walling.

Single-ply profiled metal

This cladding is sealed by suitable lapping of adjacent sheets and the use of wet-applied sealants or tapes (Figure 4.11). Thin metal sheets used in this way in the outer layer of a wall or roof are subject to large changes in temperature, from -20°C to 80°C in the UK (Section 1.6.1). The temperature movement to be accommodated at each end lap joint will depend on the length of the panel and the type and positioning of fasteners and fixings. Relative movement at the side lap joints is restricted by the mechanical overlap of the profiles. The manufacturer's advice should be followed when attaching and fixing profiled metal.

Composite panels

Constructions using these panels are normally sealed (panel-to-panel) using gaskets and proprietary connection details. Wet-applied sealants may be used to seal these panels to adjacent components such as windows or penetrations.

The outer metal ply will undergo substantial temperature changes, from -20°C to 80°C in the UK. However the inner ply is insulated from radiation and undergoes a far smaller temperature change. Composite panels expand and contract less than single-ply metal but are more likely to bow as a result of differential surface temperatures (Section 1.6.1).

Rainscreen panels

Rainscreen panels are installed with sufficient open joints to provide drainage and ventilation of the cavity behind. Horizontal joints are constructed as shown in Figure 4.14. Vertical joints may be constructed as open or sealed joints. Rainscreen panels experience large changes in temperature; for this reason, open joints are preferred. If joints are to be sealed then panels should be restrained adjacent to the joint to create a low-movement joint as shown in Figure 4.13.

In a rainscreen construction with a ventilated cavity it is necessary to seal the inner wall to form an air barrier. The inner wall may be a masonry wall as shown in Figure 4.10. Alternatively the air barrier may be an inner skin of metal panels sealed as shown in Figure 4.14.

Metal infill panels

Metal infill panels may be installed into the glazing rebates of a stick curtain wall in the same way as glazing units. They are best restrained and sealed by gasket seals.

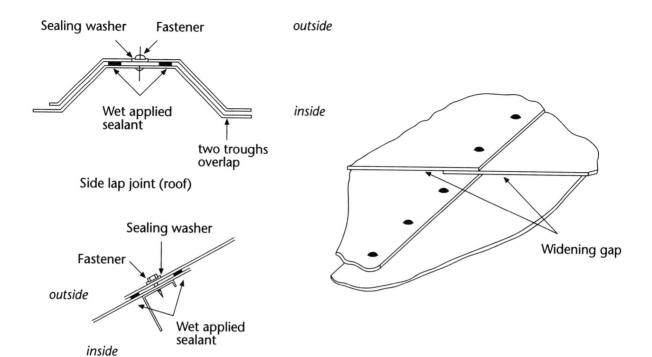

Sealing washer   Fastener   *outside*

Wet applied
sealant   *inside*

two troughs
overlap

Side lap joint (roof)

Sealing washer

Fastener

outside

Wet applied
sealant

inside

End lap joint (roof)

Widening gap

Figure 4.11 *Profiled metal walls and roofs*

Adjacent sheets are connected one to another by
stitching fasteners. Profiles should be correctly
sidelapped (often two troughs overlapped) in
accordance with the supplier's instructions.

End laps are sealed in a similar manner, however the
overlap of the sheets is not so clearly defined. The
supplier's recommendations should be followed for
overlapping sheets. Note that, for roofs, the lower
the pitch the greater the overlap required.

The joint may be sealed with a sealing strip or wet-
applied sealant. Wet-applied sealants are applied as
a bead to one surface and squashed between the
two panels as they are fastened. A single line of
sealant may be applied on the line of the fasteners.
A better result is obtained if similar seals are placed
one on each side of the line of fasteners.

Profiled metal sheeting on walls is fixed through the
trough of the profile to the framing members
supporting it. For roofing sheets, where water runs in
the troughs of the profile, fixings may be placed
through the ridges of the profile to reduce the risk of
leakage at the fixing points. This can lead to
distortion of the sheet unless it is properly supported
and opinions differ as to best practice.

Fixings and fasteners penetrating the sheeting are a
potential cause of leakage and they should be
sealed with proprietary washers. The use of a wet-
applied sealant in place of sealing washers is seldom
successful.

Figure 4.12 *Metal walls and roofs (joint
intersections)*

At joint intersections between horizontal and vertical
joints, four sheets are overlapped. At these points not
all panels can be in close contact with adjacent panels.
Vertical joints may be continued through the intersection
at constant joint width. The horizontal joint will vary in
sheet separation to create a joint of variable width. Any
wet-applied sealant or sealing strip should be selected
and applied to accommodate this increased joint width.

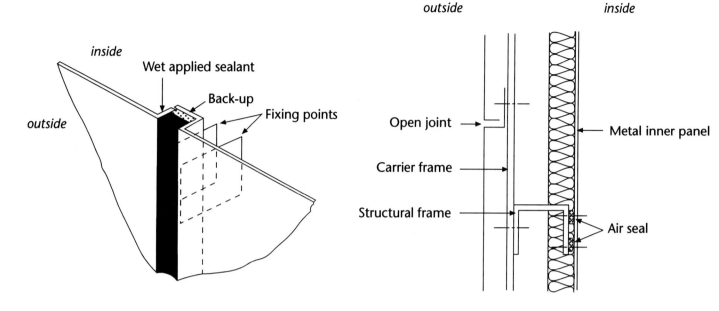

Figure 4.13 *Metal over-cladding (face-sealed)*

Figure 4.14 *Metal over-cladding (air-sealing ventilated walls)*

The panels to be sealed are generally flexible and have to be restrained immediately adjacent to the joint to create a low-movement joint. This may be achieved by fastening adjacent panels to a common support rail or to each other.

Similar considerations apply to other lightweight panels such as GFRP and high-pressure phenolic laminates.

For metal panels such as those shown, a Z-shape may be formed at the panel edge to provide a good location for the sealant system. For panels with single returns and for square-edge panels such as laminates it is more difficult to locate the back-up in the joint and obtain the correct depth of sealant. Many panels are too thin to accommodate anything other than the sealant. Such panels have to be fastened to a back rail that forms the back of the joint gap.

Because many of the panels are thin, and because of the methods of fixing them in position, it is often easier to seal them using a cellular sealing strip, either within a lapped joint or between the panels and a common back rail.

The cavity behind a face-sealed over-cladding should be drained to remove any inadvertent leakage past the sealant joints. The figure does not show the wall insulation or air barrier/inner wall.

Many over-cladding systems are proprietary systems and should be sealed in accordance with the supplier's guidance.

These walls comprise a metal over-cladding with either face-sealed or open joints, behind which is a ventilated cavity. The inner layer of these walls may also comprise a system of metal panels to form an air barrier. The air barrier should be continuous and all components of it – for instance window frames – should be sealed into the air barrier.

For walls of cassette construction and those comprising an inner wall of separate panels it is necessary to seal the panel joints of the inner layer. Panels may be sealed one to another or each to a common framing member. These sealant joints are in a protected environment and are often made using cellular sealing strips. As with other flexible panels they should be fastened in close proximity to the joints.

4.4.5   Windows and doors into walls

Joints between window/door frames and walls are a common cause of leakage. Often a single sealant joint is placed in an exposed position between a frame and the outer face of a wall, and failure of this joint leads to leakage of water into and through the wall.

Information on walls is given in Sections 4.4.1, 4.4.2, 4.4.3 and 4.4.4.

Window and door frames

Window and door frames are designed as products, but they are not self-contained in their performance. They are designed to be installed into walls in particular ways such that the air barrier of the wall and window is continuous, water drainage paths within the wall and window/door frame are co-ordinated and water is shed from the construction as a whole.

Windows using insulated glazing units are constructed with an inner gasket that is a water and air seal. The outer gasket serves to minimise water leakage into the glazing cavity between the inner and outer gaskets. This glazing cavity is drained to allow any inadvertent leakage water to flow out. The bottom rail of the window frame will be either face drained or bottom drained. The window should be sealed into the wall opening so that water can drain from the outer face of the frame or the underside of the frame as intended by the window manufacturer (Figures 4.21 and 4.22).

Some frame profiles are easier to seal into walls than others. The choice of a suitable frame profile appropriate to the wall construction will lead to a better seal that is easier to construct. Figure 4.15 illustrates good practice and is used as a key reference drawing for other figures in this section.

Fixing

Window frames are fixed in position either by using cleats as shown or by direct screwing through the frame. The use of cleats is preferred and most frame manufacturers are able to supply suitable cleats. Direct screwing through the frame may penetrate dpms or sills and may allow water to drain from, for example, the glazing rebate to the reinforcement chamber in a PVC-U window or into some other undrained cavity.

Air and water seals

Great reliance is often placed on single-line-of-defence seals at the outer face of the wall, yet these sealant systems act only as gap fillers not sealed joints. It should be assumed that water will pass these seals by seeping through porous wall materials such as brick and mortar and by leaking past a sealant system that no longer adheres to the joint faces. A secondary defence system with drained and ventilated cavities should be provided (Figures 4.17-4.20) with appropriate dpms to intercept any leakage water and direct it to the outer face of the wall as shown in Figure 4.24.

Window frames that bridge cavities in drained and ventilated walls (including masonry walls) should always have a flashing or cloak built into the head of the window opening to drain water from the cavity. This is to prevent water from falling onto the head of the window frame and then draining back to the inner face of the wall (Figures 4.23 and 4.25).

The air seal of the window should be made continuous with the air barrier in the wall by air seals between the frame and the wall air barrier. This seal should be continuous around the window. Sill joints are a common oversight when constructing a continuous air seal (Figures 4.21 and 4.22).

UK practice has been to plaster up to the window frame, but this does not form a definite air seal. A better practice, common in Scandinavian countries, is to use a sealant air seal such as the one shown in Figure 4.15. This practice is shown throughout Section 4.4.5.

Joint movement

Window-to-wall joints can be divided into two categories: low-movement joints, and movement joints that accommodate larger, calculated movements (Section 3.3).

Low movement joints

For joints between windows/doors and brickwork, blockwork or monolithic concrete panels the movement to be accommodated is low if the adjacent components are correctly restrained. Movement arises mainly from thermal movement of the window/door frame, which should be fixed to the wall in accordance with the manufacturer's recommendations. Thermal movements for window/door frames are greatest for PVC-U and least for timber frames (Section 1.6.1). Low-movement joints may be constructed as fillet joints, dimensioned as shown in Section 3.2.1. However, these are in an exposed position, and butt and lap joints are preferred for reasons of longevity of the joint.

Movement joints

Windows installed in metal walls, unitised concrete walls and rainscreens of metal or stone have to be sealed to the wall with wider and deeper joints that accommodate the calculated movement of the window/door frame, adjacent wall components and structural frame (Section 3.3 and Figures 4.23–4.33). The calculated movement will normally dictate the use of butt or lap joints.

Window assemblies

Individual windows may be built up into assemblies, either using proprietary joining mullions supplied by the window manufacturer or making use of custom-made joining mullions (Figure 4.16). Although windows are tested for watertightness in accordance with BS6375: Pt 1: 1989, joining mullions and sills are seldom included in the tests. Proprietary components forming part of a proven system will give the best seal with the least risk of failure.

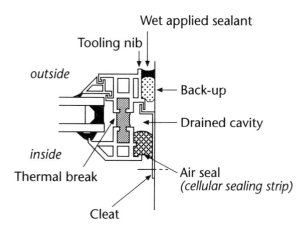

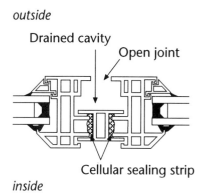

Figure 4.15 *Window/door frames into wall*

For the external seal a butt or lap joint is preferable, sealed with a cellular sealing strip or wet-applied sealant. The window/door frame must present a plane surface parallel to a surface of the wall and of sufficient extent to form a proper joint gap. The faces of the gap may be either front face of frame and rear face of wall, or edge of frame and edge of wall.

For gaps greater than 5 mm a back-up material should be used in the joint. A fillet joint may be used and should be dimensioned in accordance with Section 3.2.1.

Neat edges to sealant joints on window frames can be difficult to achieve, particularly for fillet seals. The provision of nibs on the frame can aid the tooling of sealant to a straight edge.

Frames designed specifically to accommodate a recessed seal may cause unnecessary difficulties for the sealant applicator, who may not have sufficient access to the joint to tool the sealant and achieve a good seal.

An inner air seal should be provided at the inner face of the frame. This may be made with either a wet-applied sealant or the internal plaster.

Frames may contain resins, sealants or adhesives as part of a thermal break or some form of composite construction using several framing materials. Good frame design will ensure that either these are compatible with, or do not contact, the sealants used to install the window.

The figure shows a thermally broken aluminium window frame.

Figure 4.16 *Window assemblies*

A good detail is to use a joint that is back-sealed as shown in the figure. The seals in such a joint are protected from the weather. They are more easily designed to accommodate movement and easier to construct.

If the outside joint is sealed, rather than an open joint, any cavity behind the seal should be drained. Particular attention must be given to the sealing of adjacent windows at sill level where flashing should be continuous and not impaired by framing members passing through them.

Frames should be fixed to each other or to a common mullion/transom to eliminate large movements.

Where joints of small dimension are required to accommodate movement it may be more appropriate to use a gasket to seal these joints.

The figure shows PVC-U window frames and a PVC-U mullion. PVC-U mullions normally require strengthening with steel inserts.

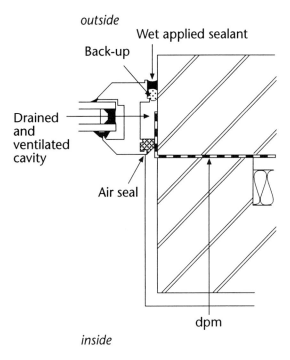

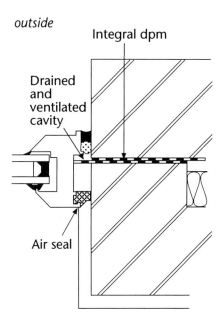

Figure 4.17 *Window/door jamb in cavity block wall (with frame in plane of outer leaf)*

The frame should preferably be sealed to the outer leaf of blockwork or brick using a butt joint. A fillet joint may be used and should be dimensioned in accordance with Section 3.2.1.

The damp-proof course should be cut back to avoid contact with the sealant system. It should, however, be returned into the jamb cavity to prevent water moving from the outer leaf to the internal finishes.

The window should be fixed either by the use of proprietary cleats supplied with the window or by screwing through the frame, but care must be taken not to penetrate the dpm.

For fixing and frame details see key Figure 4.15.

Figure 4.18 *Window/door jamb in cavity block wall (frame with integral dpm)*

These window and door frames have a flashing or dpm bonded to them. The frame is positioned so that the dpm lies in the correct plane of the wall.

It is essential that the vertical dpm extends from the window/door frame into the cavity of the wall.

There is no need for an outer weather seal, although one is sometimes provided as shown above to limit ingress of water to the jamb cavity. In the absence of an outer weather seal, considerable amounts of water may pass the outer (open) joint. Care is needed to ensure proper lapping of the vertical dpm at the sill so that this water drains out of the construction (Figure 4.24). Even when an outer seal is provided, water may enter the jamb cavity through porous block and brick or by leakage through the joint.

The window should be fixed in position using proprietary cleats supplied with the window. The use of fixing screws through the frame may damage the integral dpm.

For fixing and frame details see key Figure 4.15.

outside

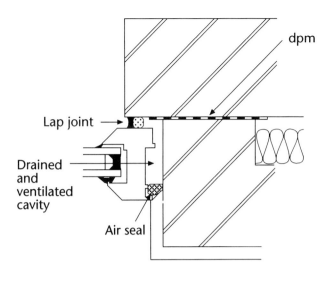

outside

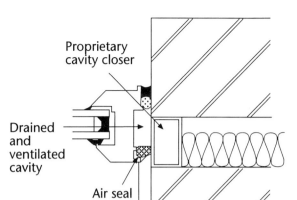

inside

inside

Figure 4.19 *Window/door jamb in cavity block wall (frame behind outer leaf)*

The frame should preferably be sealed to the inner face of the outer leaf of blockwork or brick as a lap joint using a wet-applied sealant or a cellular sealing strip.

A fillet joint may be used, but note that it will be in an exposed position. It will be an inferior seal and will deteriorate more quickly than the concealed joint shown.

The vertical dpm should not contact the sealant system and is normally kept out of the jamb cavity as shown or returned round the inner leaf.

The frame should be fixed in position using cleats or screwing directly to the outer leaf. A spacer is normally required to ensure a sufficient gap to accommodate the sealant system or avoid over-compression of the cellular sealing strip.

A detail similar to this may be used for fixing and sealing window and door frames into solid blockwork walls.

For fixing and frame details see key Figure 4.15.

Figure 4.20 *Window/door jamb in cavity block wall (proprietary cavity closer)*

The frame should be sealed to the outer leaf of the blockwork or brick preferably using a butt joint, although a fillet joint may be used.

It should be recognised that leakage may occur through the seal or around the seal through porous blockwork, brick or mortar. The window/door frame should be placed in the wall such that it overlaps the cavity closer. There should be no contact between the outer leaf of the wall and the internal finishes.

It is often not possible to fix the frame by direct screwing into the outer leaf of the wall. Cleats designed for use with a cavity closer should be used.

An air seal should be made between the frame and the inner surface of the wall. This may require a seal between the frame and cavity closer and also a seal between the closer and the inner leaf of the wall. These seals may be made using wet-applied sealants, cellular sealing strip, or an internal plaster.

For fixing and frame details see key Figure 4.15.

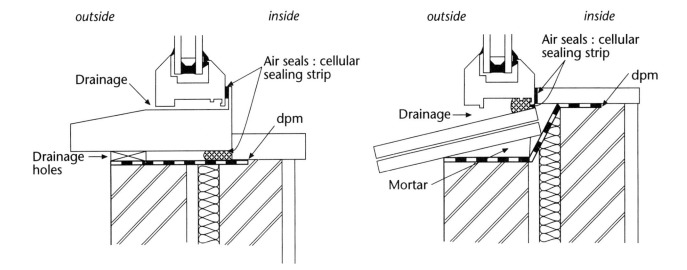

outside   inside   outside   inside

Figure 4.21 *Window sill in cavity block wall (using a sub-sill)*

Sub-sills of plastic, metal or timber may be provided as part of the window frame or as a separate item. Sub-sills that are not integral with the bottom rail of the window frame should be sealed to it. This may be achieved using a small joint sealant approved by the window supplier or by gaskets.

Sub-sills are often fixed in position by screwing through into the wall below. Any holes drilled through the sill are a potential cause of leakage into and through the wall. A small joint sealant should be used to seal screw heads to the sill.

Sub-sills are usually sealed to the outer leaf of the wall below by either bedding them on mortar as shown above or by bedding them on a bead of wet sealant. The construction of good seals is often prohibited for reasons of access. The use of a second bead of sealant or a cellular sealing strip as an air seal at the internal edge of the sill will provide a better seal.

The quality of the seal may be impaired by the poor surface of the top of the wall, particularly when installing replacement windows.

Many proprietary window systems use standard sub-sill profiles. Often these windows can only be placed in the outer leaf or mid-plane of the wall as the sills do not project forward far enough for use in the inner leaf. Large sub-sills tend to be unstable and are difficult to fix in position. Consideration should be given to the use of a sill constructed from tiles or brick as shown in Figure 4.22.

For fixing and frame details see key Figure 4.15.

Figure 4.22 *Window sill in cavity block wall (using tiles or bricks)*

The use of sloping ceramic tiles or bricks to form a window sill will provide better drainage from the foot of the window and is easier to seal against air and water ingress.

The window is sealed at its inner face to the ceramic tiles or blockwork and this provides both an air seal and a water seal. Either a wet-applied sealant or a cellular sealing strip is used to make this seal.

The outer edge of the frame is either left as an open joint or covered with a trim. This should have holes to allow drainage of the sill cavity. If a sealant joint is used at this position for aesthetic reasons, it should contain weep holes to permit drainage.

The window board is sealed to the inner face of the window frame to provide an air seal between the wall cavity and the interior of the building.

The frame member is fixed in position by screwing through into the sill below, or to the inner leaf by the use of cleats.

For fixing and frame details, see key Figure 4.15.

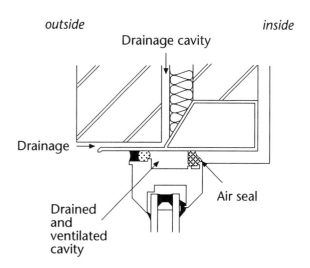

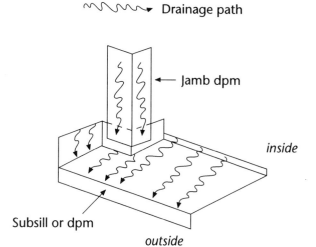

Figure 4.23 *Window/door head in cavity block wall*

Provision has to be made to intercept water in the wall cavity above the opening and drain it outwards from the wall. A dpm or flashing may be incorporated in the lintel as shown or may be provided separately. Water should be free to drain as shown or the perpend mortar joints in the outer leaf of blockwork or brick should be left open to provide drainage. The dpm or flashing should have upstands at each end (similar to the sill dpm) to prevent water flowing laterally in the wall (Figure 4.24).

The window frame should be sealed to the lintel preferably using a butt joint. Fillet joints may be used and should be in accordance with Section 3.2.1.

An air seal should be provided at the inner face of the frame using either a wet-applied sealant, cellular sealing strip, or by internal plaster, Section 4.4.5.

For fixing and frame details, see key Figure 4.15.

Figure 4.24 *Jamb/sill intersections*

All damp-proof membranes and sills should be properly lapped to drain water to the outer face of the wall and to prevent it flowing into the building or parts of the wall where it may adversely affect performance. The figure shows the requirements for dpms and sills that are properly co-ordinated.

Sills and dpms at sill level must slope to drain water outwards. An upstand at the inner face ensures no water flows inwards. Upstands at the ends will ensure that water drains off the wall and not from the end of the sill into some other part of the wall. Sills should intercept all water running down the outer surface of the vertical dpm or within a drained cavity.

Jambs should contain vertical dpms to prevent water ingress at the jamb. Any cavity between the dpm and the window frame should be drained to take away any inadvertent leakage. The jamb dpm should overlap the sill so that all water in the jamb cavity is intercepted by the sill.

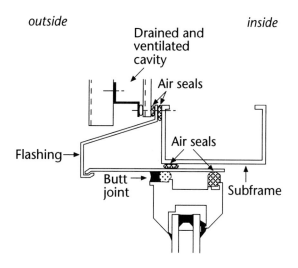

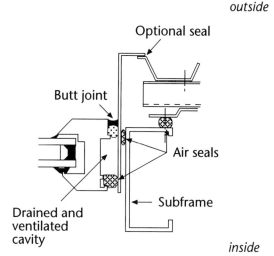

Figure 4.25 *Window head in metal wall*

The figure shows a double-skin metal wall with a cavity. Similar considerations will apply for single-skin walls and walls of metal-faced composite panels.

For a double-skin wall the inner layer should be regarded as the air barrier. An air seal should be made between the inner metal panels and the window frame. This may require each to be sealed separately to the structural subframe.

Sealants used within the wall are often cellular sealing strips. However, beads of sealant are also used trapped between fixed components.

It should be assumed that the cavity in a double-skin wall is a moist zone. Window heads should be flashed and drained to direct water from the cavity to the outer face of the wall.

Windows and doors should not be fixed direct to the cladding but to a structural frame or subframe.

Fixings that penetrate flashings are potential causes of leakage. They should be avoided or attention given to the adequate sealing of any penetrations.

Wall insulation has been omitted from the figure for clarity.

For fixing and frame details, see key Figure 4.15.

Figure 4.26 *Window jamb in metal wall*

The principles of sealing the window jamb are similar to those for the head.

A metal panel will be used to close the end of the wall cavity and provide a neat reveal to the window opening.

If, as is normally the case, the reveal panel is placed between the window frame and the wall then the panel must be sealed to both to provide a continuous air barrier. The seal to the window may be either a butt or fillet joint or a cellular sealing strip. The seal to the wall may be either a cellular sealing strip or a bead of sealant.

The reveal panel may be sealed to the outer metal leaf using a cellular sealing strip or sealant bead or may be left as an open joint.

For composite panels, systems companies often manufacture proprietary window pods or provide guidance on window installation. The joints between window and pod and between pod and panel must both provide an air and a water seal.

Wall insulation has been omitted from the figure for clarity.

For fixing and frame details, see key Figure 4.15.

outside   *inside*   *outside*   *inside*

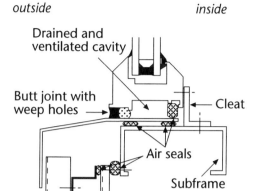

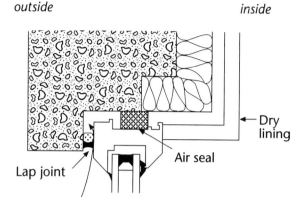

Figure 4.27 *Window sill in metal wall*

As with cavity brick walls the sill must catch any water bypassing the window-wall seals and drain it outwards from the wall.

The sill will be made as a sub-sill, either as a standard extrusion or fabricated from sheet metal. The sill has to be compatible with the drainage of the window frame. If the frame is designed so that the glazing rebate drains through the base of the frame then an appropriate drainage path is necessary at the sill in the same way as Figure 4.22. In the above illustration, weep holes are provided in the outer seal to allow drainage and an air seal is provided at the inner face of the window frame.

The bottom member of the window frame and the sill should be securely fastened to a subframe in accordance with the manufacturer's instructions. Any fasteners that penetrate the sill should be suitably sealed to it.

The underside of the sill should be sealed to the inner layer of the wall to provide a continuous air barrier. For cavity walls, the underside of the sill is not normally sealed to the outer skin of the wall. An open joint provides additional ventilation of the wall cavity.

Wall insulation has been omitted from the figure for clarity.

For fixing and frame details, see key Figure 4.15.

Figure 4.28 *Window head in concrete wall*

The window frame may be fixed behind a rebate as shown or fixed into a square-edged opening.

The figure shows a precast concrete panel. In-situ concrete is normally formed with a square edge.

An air barrier should be clearly identified and be continuous. The concrete wall may provide an adequate air barrier on its own or in combination with internal finishes. However, dry linings are seldom effective air barriers and an air seal must be provided at the head of the window. Its exact position will depend on the internal finishes and detailing of the panel.

The use of separate water and air seals, as shown above, with a cavity reduces the risk of water leakage. The cavity may or may not be drained and ventilated depending on the seals and the sill detail.

Air seals may be made using either butt or lap joints, with cellular sealing strips or wet-applied sealants.

A single air/water seal may be acceptable in precast panels as very good tolerances can be achieved in the construction of openings, which by their nature are also rigid openings. A good sealant joint of uniform cross-section can normally be made, particularly if the joint is made under factory conditions.

A similar detail is used for the window jamb.

For fixing and frame details, see key Figure 4.15.

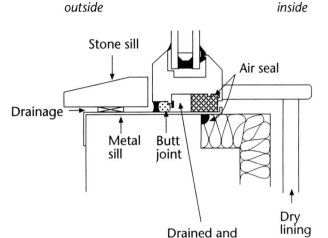

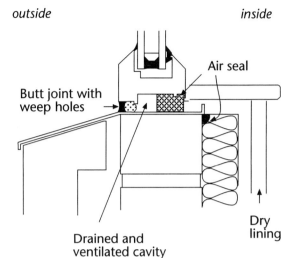

Figure 4.29 *Window sill in concrete wall*

The bottom member of the window frame is attached
securely to the wall either by cleats or screwing and
an air and water seal is formed using a butt joint with
either a wet-applied sealant or a cellular sealing strip.

The glazing rebate of the frame should be drained to
the outer face of the frame unless the cavity is
drained. The drainage should occur on the outside
of any window-wall sealant joints, or weep tubes
should be provided in the sealant joint. If weep tubes
are used then a secondary air seal must be provided
all around the window to create a continuous air
barrier. As with the head detail, a single line of
defence is often considered satisfactory for precast
panels.

A sill is provided using a sub-sill with or without a
concrete/stone sill as shown. Concrete/stone sills
may be used to conceal the joint, but they must not
impair the drainage of the window frame. A sub-sill
placed between the precast concrete panel and the
window frame should be sealed to both to form an air
barrier.

For fixing and frame details, see key Figure 4.15.

Figure 4.30 *Window sill in wall of small precast
concrete units*

Precast units may be smaller panels hung from a steel
strongback as part of a panellised construction or used
as spandrel walls, possibly incorporating a masonry
inner leaf. These panels may experience considerable
movement and window frames should be fastened to
the steel frame of a strongback or to a masonry inner
leaf as shown above, not to small concrete units no
bigger than the window itself.

Air and water seals should be made between the
window frame and the inner wall elements to which it is
securely fixed. Any additional joints between the
precast units and the window frame or sill are either left
open or sealed using butt joints with wet-applied sealant
or cellular sealing strip. These joints have to
accommodate movement of the precast unit relative to
the window.

Similar considerations apply for units of dimensioned
stone.

For fixing and frame details, see key Figure 4.15.

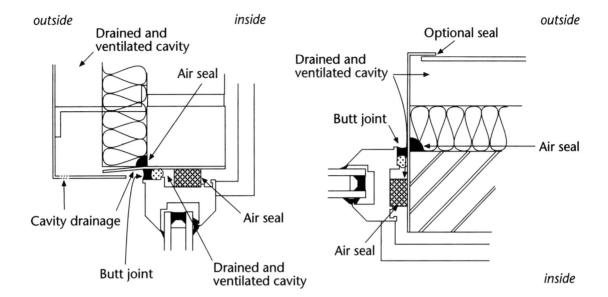

Figure 4.31 *Window head in rainscreen over-cladding*

Rainscreen over-clad walls have a comparatively flexible outer layer of metal, stone or laminated panels. Window and door frames should be fixed to the inner structural support of the rainscreen: either a masonry wall or structural subframe supporting the over-cladding.

Normally, no seal is made between the rainscreen panels and the window frame. Openings at the head assist ventilation of the cavity.

The inner layer of the wall is the only air barrier. All window frames should be sealed into this. The seal between the frame and the air barrier may be made using a butt joint with wet-applied sealant or cellular sealing strip, or a fillet joint.

For fixing and frame details, see key Figure 4.15.

Figure 4.32 *Window jamb in rainscreen over-cladding*

Window frame jambs are designed using the same principles as described in Figure 4.31. The edge of the cavity behind the rainscreen is closed with a reveal panel.

The reveal panel may be a single panel covering the jamb or may be part of a complete window pod. Some over-cladding systems require a sealed joint between the window frame and reveal, others permit an open joint. For complete window pods the manufacturer's advice should be sought.

If a sealant joint is to be made between the reveal and the window frame then they should be fixed to produce a low-movement joint. The reveal panel is normally trapped between the frame and the inner wall as shown. It should be sealed to both to form a continuous air barrier.

When complete window pods are used, gaskets may be used to seal the window to the pod. An air seal still has to be made between the window pod and inner wall air barrier and this is best made using a wet-applied sealant or cellular sealing strip.

For fixing and frame details, see key Figure 4.15.

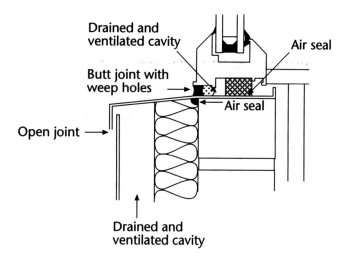

outside   inside

Drained and ventilated cavity

Air seal

Butt joint with weep holes →

← Air seal

Open joint →

Drained and ventilated cavity

Figure 4.33 *Window sill in rainscreen over-cladding*

A sub-sill is provided. This may be a standard profile, in which case it may form part of a complete window pod, or be fabricated from sheet metal.

Water inadvertently entering the glazing rebate of the window frame should be drained through holes in the frame. This water may be drained forward through weep holes in the sealant onto the sill, as shown, or drained into the drained cavity of the rainscreen.

Either the window frame is sealed direct to the inner wall air barrier or both are sealed to the sill to create a continuous air barrier. There is normally no seal between the sill and the outer rainscreen as for a window sill in a metal wall, Figure 4.27.

As with jamb details, manufacturers' advice should be sought if complete window pods including a sill are to be used.

For fixing and frame details, see key Figure 4.15.

4.4.6   Stick system curtain walls and slope glazing

The sealing of stick system curtain walling to an adjacent element is very similar to the sealing of windows into walls. However, the framing members are larger and the potential for movement is greater. Dimensional deviations are also potentially greater.

The joints may be single face-sealed joints or double joints with an outer open joint and a ventilated cavity. As with all other joints, air seals are necessary to ensure a continuous air barrier. Note that air leakage between ventilated cavities in the adjacent construction and the interior of the building should be prevented.

All curtain wall system companies produce standard details and guidance relating to their proprietary system and their advice should be sought.

Movement

Stick system curtain walls and slope glazing systems contain gasket seals at every glass-frame joint and are able to accommodate large out-of-plane shear movements by small movements of each and every joint.

Thermal expansion/contraction can cause large movements at the edge of stick system curtain walls and slope glazing unless the framing members are separated by expansion-contraction joints within the curtain wall. There are two main causes of structural movement between the curtain wall and an adjacent element. Where the head of the wall interfaces with a roof slab (Figure 4.36) the roof will move relative to the mullions that are longitudinally stiff (Section 1.6). At the side edge of the wall mullions may bend, giving rise to differential out-of-plane movement, and at the side edge of slope glazing similar movements arise due to snow load as well as wind load (Figure 4.38).

All joints around the perimeter of a stick system curtain wall or slope glazing system should either be designed as movement joints (Section 3.3) or constructed as 'low-movement' joints and adequately restrained (Figures 4.34–4.38).

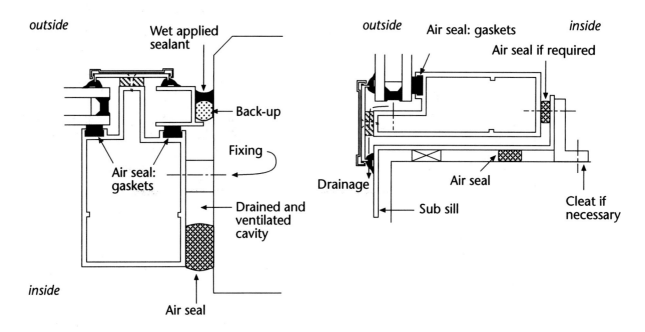

Figure 4.34 *Curtain wall edge detail*

Some curtain walls include end mullions that provide a standard glazing detail on one side and present a flat surface on the other to form a suitable joint gap. More normally, a curtain walling system will comprise only symmetrical mullion profiles that are also used as an end mullion. In this case, a small infill is inserted and sealed to the wall as shown.

For some systems a narrow infill can be gripped in the glazing rebate and sealed without fixing to the wall, as shown. In this case the curtain walling mullion should be fixed to the wall at intervals to limit movement of the joint. Wider infills than that shown may be used and should be fixed to the wall to reduce movement at the sealant joint.

Figure 4.35 *Curtain wall sill detail*

Curtain walling stick systems comprise a whole range of standard profiles. The sill detail is usually a framing member incorporating a sill or a special box section framing member incorporating a glazing rebate and mounted above a sub-sill as shown above. The use of a standard glazing transom for this purpose is seldom successful.

Particular attention should be given to the drainage of the wall. The glazing rebate will often be a drained and ventilated cavity. Drainage from the rebate should not be restricted by frame-to-sill or frame-to-floor/wall seals.

Some curtain walling systems allow for inadvertent leakage past glazing gaskets by drainage through the transoms and down the inside of the mullions. With these systems, the base of the mullion should be detailed to drain water out of the mullion to the outer face of the wall.

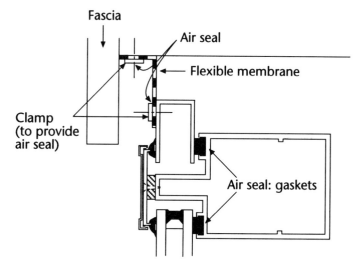

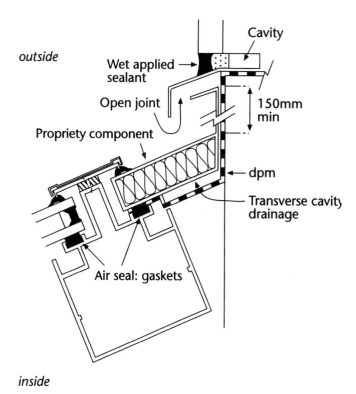

outside   inside

Fascia

Air seal

Flexible membrane

Clamp (to provide air seal)

Air seal: gaskets

Cavity

outside

Wet applied sealant

Open joint

Propriety component

150mm min

dpm

Transverse cavity drainage

Air seal: gaskets

inside

Figure 4.36 *Stick system curtain wall head detail*

For stick system curtain walling this is likely to be the boundary that experiences greatest movement, particularly where a lightweight roof is used. On large glazing screens, such as walls to swimming pools, all of the vertical movement of the wall may be accommodated at this joint.

Where movement can be limited, a detail similar to the edge detail (Figure 4.34) may be used. If greater movement has to be accommodated then a flexible joint is necessary. Different manufacturers adopt different methods of sealing the head of a curtain wall. A commonly used and successful approach is to use a flexible membrane fastened and sealed to the roof and the head of the wall as shown above. This is protected by a fascia board. The inner air seal is provided by the glazing gaskets and the flexible membrane.

Other methods of sealing include the use of two components that are slotted and incorporate brush seals to provide an air seal. A water seal is not needed if a sufficiently deep fascia/overhang is provided to protect the joint.

Figure 4.37 *Slope glazing head detail*

The glazing bars of slope glazing systems are supported at the head and movement of this joint is small. However, the joint is in a highly exposed place on the building and failure leads to immediate water leakage. For these reasons a flashed joint is used.

On new-build projects, a dpm should pass right through the wall to intercept all seepage water within the wall cavities. Frequently, slope glazing is joined to an existing wall as part of a building extension. In this case, a flashing is inserted into a slot cut into the wall. This should be of sufficient depth to intercept seepage in the wall and drainage water in any cavities.

Water seals at the joint should be co-ordinated with the water seals and drainage of the slope glazing. Air seals, if provided, should form a continuous air barrier between the roof and the air barrier of the wall.

Water seeping down the wall should not be trapped by the dpm but should be drained out of the wall. It should not be trapped behind any sealant joint. Sealant joints should incorporate weep tubes, or a porous joint filler should be used.

An air seal is not necessary for slope glazing that is itself air-permeable (patent glazing).

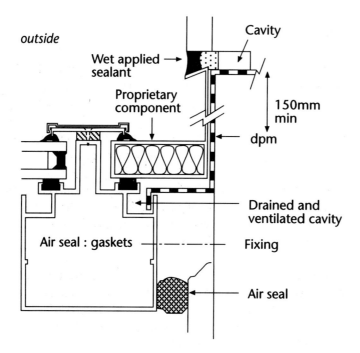

outside

Cavity

Wet applied → sealant

Proprietary component

150mm min

dpm

Drained and ventilated cavity

Air seal : gaskets

Fixing

Air seal

inside

Figure 4.38 *Slope glazing edge detail*

Deflections at the edge of a slope glazing system (span/200) are usually greater than at its head. They may be reduced by fixing the edge glazing bar to the adjacent wall.

The vertical upstand at the edge of the glazing system should be sufficient to contain any water draining down the slope glazing. The proprietary flashing will normally be stepped to co-ordinate with the courses of brick or blockwork.

Water seals should be co-ordinated with the water seals in the glazing system. The proprietary component may form a gutter to prevent water running onto the glazing.

Dpms and sealant joints should be constructed as for the head detail (Figure 4.37).

Similar considerations apply to other roof systems.

4.4.7   Parapet cappings

The tops of parapet walls have to be protected with a capping of stone or metal. Stone cappings used on blockwork or masonry walls may be sealed using wet-applied sealants. (Section 4.4.3 gives some advice on sealing joints between stone.)

Parapet cappings to metal or brick walls may be fabricated from sheet metal. For many metal walls they will be supplied as a component of a proprietary system.

For proprietary systems, guidance is available from manufacturers. Ideally, cappings should be fastened using concealed fixings. Fixing through the top of the capping creates a site for possible leakage and these penetrations are unlikely to be sealed successfully using wet-applied sealants.

Metal parapet panels undergo large thermal movements and are comparatively flexible. They should either be adequately restrained to prevent temperature movement or joints should be designed to accommodate all calculated movement (Figure 4.39). Temperature ranges of -20°C to 80°C may be experienced in the UK (Section 1.6.1). Further guidance on the sealing of metal panels is given in Section 4.4.4.

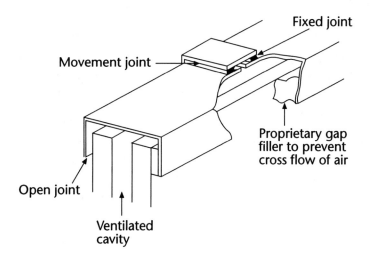

Figure 4.39 *Metal parapets*

*For a double-skin wall with a ventilated cavity, the
parapet should allow ventilation. An open joint is
provided between the parapet capping and the
external layer of the wall for this purpose. An air seal
is normally provided between the inner layer of the
wall and the capping to create an air barrier and
reduce airflow through the open, outer, joint.
Proprietary gap-fillers shaped to match profiled
sheets are frequently used at this location.*

*A good joint can be achieved by butting adjacent
capping panels end to end and placing a covering
panel over the joint as shown in the figure. Joints
may be sealed using either wet-applied sealants or a
cellular sealing strip.*

*Some capping panels can be lapped over each other
at their ends. The resulting joint gap is narrow and
the joint should be fixed, as it will not accommodate
movement. However, fixing may be difficult unless
the panel is penetrated.*

4.4.8   Service penetrations

Penetrations should be minimised because they cause a complex geometry that is difficult to seal. Ducts, flues and similar penetrations through the building envelope have to be sealed to prevent water leakage and unacceptable air leakage. The sealed joints are normally constructed as low-movement joints with the duct/flue connected to the wall, but they may be designed as movement joints to accommodate calculated movement (Section 3.3 and Figure 4.40). The joints also have to accommodate dimensional deviations (Section 3.4).

For flues and other hot surfaces the sealant systems and other components of the joint have to be tolerant of heat, or insulated by a suitable collar. Any collars or similar fittings used should be fixed either to the flue/duct or to the wall/roof and not 'float' between two movement joints (Figure 4.41).

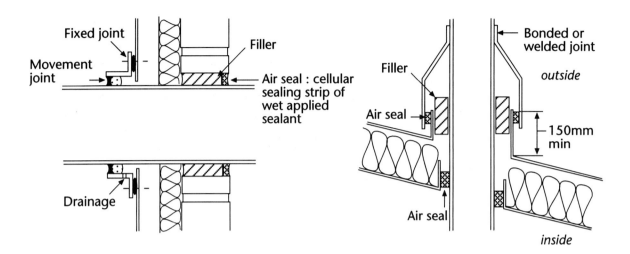

outside   inside

Fixed joint

Movement joint

Filler

Air seal : cellular sealing strip of wet applied sealant

Drainage

Filler

Air seal

Air seal

Bonded or welded joint

outside

150mm min

inside

Figure 4.40 *Service penetration through wall*

Penetrations through walls should be avoided or minimised. The service pipe or duct must be separately supported and fixed. The sealant should not be expected to provide any support.

A filler is generally required and expanded foams are frequently used. Care should be taken that they have fully expanded and that no further gas is being released before placing sealant over them.

An outer seal may be obtained by placing a collar around the duct or pipe. The collar should be fastened to the wall or pipe or both. The joint gaps should then be sealed as fixed or movement joints accordingly, as shown above.

Water falling in the cavity should not be directed towards the inner leaf by the pipe or duct and drainage holes to the outside should be provided.

An air seal should be made between the inner leaf and the pipe or duct to prevent air leakage from the drained and ventilated cavity into the building.

For fire-rated walls it will be necessary to maintain the fire resistance of the wall. Fire-rated sealants or intumescent protection may be necessary.

Figure 4.41 *Penetration through metal roof*

Penetrations through roofs are best avoided.

Where a flue, pipe or duct has to pass through a roof a combination of sealant joint and flashing is required.

The best method of keeping the water out is to use a skirt attached to the pipe as shown in the figure. In the absence of a skirt, wet-applied sealant joints are difficult to construct and are prone to water lying on them. Failure of the sealant joints will almost invariably lead to leakage into the building and impairment of the building fabric. An air seal may be provided under a skirt to reduce the airflow and prevent whistling. This is best done with a cellular sealing strip.

As an alternative to a flashing, a hole can be cut in the roof sheet and an upstand fabricated that is fastened and sealed to the sheet as a fixed joint. Either a circular gasket, beads of wet-applied sealant or cellular sealing strip are used to make this joint. The pipe or duct is sealed into the upstand created to produce an air and water seal.

An air seal has to be made between the pipe and the inner skin (air barrier). This is best achieved by using a suitable collar or upstand and a cellular sealing strip.

5   Installation

5.1   GENERAL

Good joint design, correct choice of sealant system and good specification alone cannot ensure satisfactory performance of a sealant joint. All of the time spent on design of the joint gap, selection of a sealant system and specification will have been wasted if the gap is not properly constructed and prepared to accept the sealant system. It is also essential to ensure that the constituent parts of the sealant system are handled correctly and applied to a high standard, preferably by a properly trained installer. A first step to ensuring a high standard of installation is to employ only installers registered in accordance with ISO9000.

This section of the guide deals with responsible site installation of sealant systems into joints in building envelopes. The advice may be divided into four broad headings: health and safety, storage and use of materials, workmanship and techniques, and planning and management. Further information is available in CIRIA *SP80, Manual on good sealant application.*

Legislation on health and safety and the introduction of the CDM (Construction, Design and Management) Regulations require all those concerned with design and construction, including sealant applicators, to manage and plan contracts in such a way as to ensure safety to themselves and others. It should be realised that effort expended on the thorough planning of a job will be paid back many times over in terms of rework avoided, reduced waste of material and efficient progress of work. It will also lead to a well-run contract under which the optimum quality and performance are obtained from the design and the sealant system.

5.2   PRELIMINARY WORK

5.2.1   Quality management

A project-specific quality plan should be produced following the principles and guidelines of ISO9000 to demonstrate how the site installation of sealant systems will be implemented from award of contract to completion. It should cover the programme, sequence of work and required inspection records. It is important to ensure that the quality plan is not simply a paper production exercise but does result in proper inspections and quality control at all stages.

The quality procedures should include inspections at all key stages of the contract. In particular it should include inspection at the following stages:

- construction of the joint
- prior to application
- following installation of back-up material
- application of primer
- inspection of applied sealant
- following clean-up.

It should also include:

- control of materials   -   availability on site
  - approved/specified material
  - storage
- control of material residue, empty cartridges, containers, etc.

Inspections may be undertaken by the company undertaking the work, by the client in the case of work by a main contractor or by a main contractor in the case of work by a subcontractor. Alternatively, a third party, such as a consultant or certifying body, may undertake inspection. Responsibility for inspection of work will depend on the form of contract being used and the companies involved. The level of inspection and responsibility for inspection should be established at the tender stage.

The effectiveness of quality procedures depends not only on inspection but also on the methods of recording inspections, procedures for registering and reporting non-compliance, and procedures to ensure that errors do not recur. A quality plan should include the following information:

- name of quality manager for the contract
- names of other key personnel
- procedure for registering and reporting non-compliance
- inspection procedure to be used at each stage of the work, as given above
- check-lists and reporting forms
- list of products to be applied
- product information
- stock control and storage procedures
- procedures for carrying out and inspecting remedial work.

Quality documentation – including the quality plan, all completed check-lists and inspection forms, and all documentation showing the materials supplied and installed – should be available for inspection at any time during the contract. The Association of Sealant Applicators publishes a *Site inspection audit check-list*. This is used to record details of the contract, transfer of information, materials to be used, site conditions and access, equipment used, safety equipment, materials on site, inspection and protection of work.

Quality documentation can have an important role to play after the completion of the work. Inspection records and other site records, for instance the work of a particular individual, use of substandard materials or adverse weather conditions, may help to trace the cause of subsequent joint failure. This information can be used to plan appropriate remedial work, which may then be limited in extent. It is good practice to keep quality documentation beyond the duration of the contract. A period of 10 years would be appropriate for many contracts.

A quality management system must include procedures for amending the documentation in the light of any remedial work that arises.

5.2.2   Method statements

Method statements, whether required by a particular contract or not, are a necessary tool to ensure that larger jobs are well planned and executed. They are increasingly required from subcontractors for many operations on construction sites as their value becomes recognised by main contractors. Forward planning in a formal way will avoid delays for the applicator, the imposition of penalties for late completion, and the problems and costs of providing additional access, and will reduce material wastage.

A method statement sets out how the contractor is implementing a quality plan and complying with health and safety legislation, the CDM Regulations and any other requirements set out in documentation specific to the contract. A method statement should not be just a list of activities, but should describe the method of working at each stage.

A method statement relating to sealant application might include:

- programme of work
- sequence of work
- site access requirements for the work
- method of access to work
- supply of specified materials
- storage of materials
- method of working – preparation
                       – application
- equipment to be used
- cleaning of equipment
- disposal of waste
- quality procedures
- weather and temperature conditions suitable for sealant application
- co-ordination of work with others
- key personnel.

A method statement has to relate to a specific job and should be appropriate for the scale of work to be undertaken. The need for a method statement and the information to be included on it should be discussed and agreed by all relevant parties at the tender stage. A method statement for sealant application has to be co-ordinated with those of the main contractor and other subcontractors. The main contractor or management contractor has to make an input to it. Method statements developed by either party independently are unlikely to lead to the successful completion of a contract.

The use of a method statement showing a programme and sequence of work can help to avoid contract intimidation caused by, for instance, the premature removal of scaffolding.

5.2.3   Survey and inspect

Before starting application work, a proper inspection of the site and measurement of the joints to be sealed should be made by the applicator. On a reseal contract this will take place early on and may have been done before tender. On a new-build contract it is equally important but it will normally take place only shortly before sealing work begins. There are two important aspects to be considered at this stage of the contract: the constructed joints to be sealed should be checked for compliance with design intent, and arrangements for access and storage of materials should be checked.

Inspection of joints

Joints should be checked for dimension and substrate quality. Narrow joints may not be large enough to accept the sealant system and sealing them may result in the sealant being over-stressed as a result of excessive movement. Joints that are too wide may require a different back-up, will need more sealant to fill them and, if sealed, may sag during application or in use. Joints that taper may create greater problems. In all cases the joint's performance should be reconsidered and, if appropriate, referred back to the designer. Joints that are too shallow or have substrates out of plane may not allow the full depth of sealant to be, with the subsequent risk of cohesive or adhesive. It may be possible to reduce the overall depth of the sealant system by using a different back-up such as a bond-breaker tape rather than a foam strip. Again, the applicator should consult the designer. Where gap dimensions are incorrect it may be possible to achieve the intended performance by the use of a higher-grade sealant after consultation with the specifier/designer. Joint surfaces should have been checked by the main contractor to ensure that they are as specified. Joints should be inspected for stability in the case of masonry and concrete, and for contamination in all cases. This will enable the applicator to bring appropriate equipment and materials on site for cleaning the joints.

Joints should be inspected visually. A piece of transparent adhesive tape may be used as a better test for the presence of dust. The tape is applied to the surface and any dust will be evident on the tape as it is peeled away. Non-porous surfaces should be wettable – water placed on the surface should spread and not collect in droplets.

Checking access and storage facilities

The sealant applicator should ensure, before starting work on site, that suitable storage facilities exist and that appropriate access to the joints is available. In particular the applicator should consider whether the work of other subcontractors prevents access. Does fixed scaffolding prevent access to the joints? Scaffolding stages should be spaced so that operatives do not have to over-reach to seal joints, nor should joints be at too great a height above each scaffold stage. Above all, the timing of the work should be discussed with the main contractor and co-ordinated with other trades using the same access. The access has to be suited to the sealant system to be used. If the sequence of work is clean, prime, install back-up and apply sealant, and time has to be allowed for materials to cure, then the sealant applicator will be moving over an area of several square metres of the building in any one period. Access from a mechanical platform may not give sufficient flexibility of movement, particularly if the work is to progress horizontally across a single-storey height.

Protection from debris and contamination by other trades during application and during the cure period should be provided (Section 5.3.10).

5.2.4   Health and safety

Issues of safety regarding the sealing of joints in the building envelope may be divided into two categories: those relating to work on building sites and at height, and those relating to the use of dangerous substances. This guide cannot give a detailed and authoritative review of all safety issues but gives an overview of the issues and references to authoritative publications on health and safety. Section 2.5.6 describes health and safety concerns in greater depth.

The principal pieces of legislation governing safety that affect the installation of sealant systems are:

- the CDM (Construction, Design and Management) Regulations, 1994
- the CHIP2 Chemicals (Hazard information and packaging for supply) Regulations, 1994 – information approved for the classification and labelling of substances and preparations dangerous for supply
- the COSHH (Control of Substances Hazardous to Health) Regulations, 1988.

All sealant systems are designed to be safe in use if applied correctly. However, most chemicals are potentially dangerous and the instructions for use should be followed. The principal problem lies with solvent cleaning of the substrates and solvents released by primers. The cured product is not hazardous, but byproducts released during application and skin contact with uncured sealants can be a hazard.

The storage, handling and use of all sealants and primers are covered by the CHIP2 Regulations. All materials must be labelled at the point of manufacture. If materials are repackaged or decanted into other containers the regulations require that they again be labelled with the original information. All manufacturers are required to provide health and safety information relating to the use of their products, and these should be available on site at all times.

The precautions to be observed on site will differ from material to material. Solvents used for cleaning give rise to particular problems. These include:

- flammability in use
- flammability in storage
- inhalation of vapours.

A few sealants also have solvents in them. They can be identified from labelling information.

All sealants, including water borne sealants, should be checked to ensure they do not give rise to problems associated with:

- skin contact
- eye contact.

Manufacturers' literature should always be consulted, but a useful guide to the safe use of sealants on site is *Safe handling of adhesives and sealants in industry: a guide for users and safety officers*, BASA.

Further guidance is provided by CIRIA *Report 125 A guide to the Control of Substances Hazardous to Health in Construction* and CIRIA *Special Publication SP90, Site Safety Handbook.*

The requirements of the CDM Regulations are described in Section 3.1.6.

5.3   SITE OPERATIONS

5.3.1   The effects of weather

All site work is dependent on weather conditions and ambient temperature. Sealants should only be used within the range of temperatures stated by the manufacturer – normally 5°C and rising is the minimum and 40°C is the maximum. They should be stored within the temperature ranges stated by the manufacture. Sealants and primers that are applied at too low a temperature may be more viscous, will be difficult to place and compact and will have an increased cure time. Those that are applied at too high a temperature may cure too quickly to allow proper placement and compaction. Sealants become less viscous at higher temperatures and the sealant is more likely to slump in the joint. Surfaces in direct sunlight may reach temperatures as high as 80°C. Application of primers and sealants to such hot surfaces is unlikely to give a proper cure and adhesion of the sealant system, if indeed the primer can be applied at such high temperatures without it flash-drying.

Joints are designed to be sealed when the components of the building envelope lie within a certain temperature range, normally 5°C to 40°C. Note that this is not the air temperature but the temperature of the components to be joined. Joints sealed at temperatures outside the intended temperature range will not allow adequate movement and are likely to be distressed or damaged by future temperature changes.

Sealants with a cure period measured in hours may undergo winter night cooling during the cure period. The sealant may then cure with the joint at full extension and fail under a subsequent joint contraction. Timing of the application should take this into account.

All surfaces to be sealed should be dry. This may be difficult to achieve during wet weather. A particular problem can be the presence of frost on surfaces to be sealed; this may happen at air temperatures in the range -10°C to 5°C. Frost may persist after the air temperature has risen. Condensation may form on cold surfaces. Removal of condensation by heating has little effect, as it will re-form. Application should not begin until the temperature has risen sufficiently for the surfaces to be dried.

The recording of air and surface temperatures and weather conditions is recommended.

5.3.2   Inspecting joints

All joints should have been inspected for depth, width and stability of the joint surfaces before beginning any sealing work on site, or as soon as possible thereafter. It is good practice to inspect joints to be sealed at the beginning of the day they are to be sealed and to anticipate any further problems of cleaning and preparing the joints (Section 5.2.1).

5.3.3   Cleaning of joints

All joints must be cleaned before installation of the sealant system to ensure proper adhesion between the substrate and the sealant system. Cleaning should remove all dust, oil, grease, surface water and surface dirt.

Non-porous surfaces such as metal and glass may be cleaned either mechanically or chemically. Joints may simply be swept clean or mechanically cleaned with abrasives or wire brushes followed by sweeping or blowing out to remove dust and debris. When compressed air is used it should be free from oil and water. When sweeping or blowing out joints, work should start at the top and progress downwards to avoid re-contamination of the joint. Solvents used to clean surfaces chemically should not leave a residue on the surface. Solvents such as methyl ethyl ketone (MEK) and acetone are suitable; white spirit should be 98%. Kerosene or petrol-based products are not suitable. Sealant manufacturers' literature should list suitable cleaners. Solvent should be applied with a clean, lint-free cloth and wiped dry with a separate dry cloth. Surfaces should not simply be left to dry in the air, as contaminants will be redeposited on the surface. Cloths should be appropriately discarded when they become soiled. The use of white or light-coloured cloths is recommended so that soiling can be seen.

Porous materials such as concrete should be adequately cured before joints are sealed (this normally takes 28 days). The surfaces of the joint should be cleaned where necessary by wire brushing, grinding, or grit blasting to provide a clean and sound surface. Compressed air used to blow away dust and particles from a joint should be free from oil and water.

Cleaning of a joint before resealing should ensure that all previously applied sealant is completely removed unless the method statement confirms that the existing and new sealants are compatible. Guidance on compatibility of residues is given in *Resealing of Buildings – a Guide to Good Practice,* R Woolman and A Hutchinson, 1994.

5.3.4   Masking

Masking may be used to protect adjacent areas but is more commonly used to produce a clean line and give a neat appearance. The need for masking will depend in part on the skill of the individual applying the sealant and in part on the shape and location of the joint and the materials to be joined. Joints against concrete with chamfered corners or window frames with nibs and recesses intended to define the joint edge may not need masking. A joint between two flush metal panels will almost certainly require masking. The use of a dark sealant between light coloured porous stones will require masking to avoid marking of the adjacent panels. However, masking tape will not adhere well to all stonework. Masking and priming are described in Section 2.3.3.

Masking tape is the most widely used tape. Ideally it should be applied in single, full-length strips. For non-porous surfaces it is good practice to mask the joint before priming and to remove it immediately after tooling the applied sealant. For porous surfaces, masking prior to priming can lead to staining and adhesion of the tape.

5.3.5   Priming

The sealant system selected may or may not require a primer. When required by the specification the primer is an essential part of the sealant system and it should be applied as recommended by the manufacturer. Primers condition the surface to improve adhesion of the sealant. Primers are described fully in Section 2.2.3. The primer to be used will differ from sealant to sealant and surface to surface. Primers are formulated to work with particular sealants and must be supplied only by that sealant's manufacturer.

Primers should not be considered to be a substitute for good cleaning of the joint. They should be applied to clean, dry, well-prepared surfaces. They should not be applied to frosty substrates. Some primers are formulated to work on damp surfaces and the manufacturer's instructions should be followed.

Primers may be wiped or brushed onto the surface. Their presence can be observed as a darkening of porous surfaces. On non-porous surfaces the primer should be applied sparingly as too much primer may affect the sealant bond. Primer should be applied only to the joint interfaces.

Primer material for use should be transferred to a working container not used direct from the original container. This prevents contamination of the bulk material. Spare primer should not be returned to the original container. When wiping primer onto a surface it is good practice to pour the primer on to the cloth. Dipping the cloth in to the primer will spread contaminants into the primer and onto other areas of the joint.

Primers have to cure fully if they are to be effective and provide the required adhesion of the sealant. Instructions on the primer will indicate the curing time. To avoid contamination, primed surfaces should not be left exposed for too long. It is inadvisable to prime too great a length of joint at one time as sealant application may be delayed due to weather or other unforeseen circumstances. It may be necessary to reapply primer to surfaces that have been primed and left exposed to the weather. Some primers can be over-primed, but others must be removed before the surfaces are reprimed. The manufacturer's instructions should be followed.

5.3.6   Back-up placement

Back-up material may be installed before or after priming. Installation after priming can lead to the primer being wiped from the surface of the joint. Placing the back-up before priming can lead to the primer contaminating the back-up, which may cause adhesion to the sealant and create a joint bonded on three sides. The position and orientation of the joint will also affect the sequence of working. For non-porous surfaces and when using bond-breaker tapes it is normal to prime before installing the back-up material.

Commonly used back-up materials are closed-cell polyethylene or polyurethane foams in the form of hoses, rods or cut rectangles – fully described in Section 2.3.2. Back-up material should be of the type, quality, size and shape given in the specification. It must be compatible with the sealant to avoid adhesion between the sealant and the back-up and to avoid staining through the sealant. Some rectangular foam back-up strips have a skin on one surface to prevent adhesion to the sealant and these strips have to be correctly orientated in the joint. The back-up material also has to be compatible with the cleaner and primer being used.

Back-up strip of round or rectangular section should be compressed by between 25% and 50% when inserted in the joint. This will ensure that the back-up remains in place during sealant application and tooling. In the case of circular sections, great care must be taken to ensure the correct shape of the back-up and the correct cross section for the sealant. It is very easy to obtain the wrong configuration from a circular rod due to twisting. Twisting of rectangular back-up is more pronounced and easily recognised.

Back-up should be inserted into the joint to the correct depth using a blunt instrument that does not damage the back-up. This may also be used to gauge the depth of the prepared joint. Nevertheless, the closed-cell foam may still be ruptured by the tool or rough surfaces. Leaving the installed back-up uncovered for an hour before applying the sealant will generally allow any gases released from the closed-cell foam to escape. Back-up material should not be stretched during insertion in the joint as this will change its shape and it will not be correctly compressed in the joint gap. It should not be twisted when in place, as this will change the profile of the sealant and may cause weakness and potential premature failure.

Not all joints are of sufficient depth to require back-up. Providing there is sufficient depth of sealant a bond-breaker tape must be used to ensure that the sealant does not adhere to the back of the joint recess. Self-adhesive polyethylene tapes may be used with most sealants. Other tapes may be suitable for use with some sealants. The sealant manufacturer's advice should be sought on the suitability of bond-breaker materials.

5.3.7   Mixing

Sealants may be one or multi-part products. Multi-part materials must be uniformly blended together immediately before application. These sealants begin to cure as soon as they are mixed and in this state are only usable for a limited period of time. Sealant that has cured beyond the recommended usable life will not properly wet the joint surfaces and may lead to an adhesion failure. The application life of the sealant given in the manufacturer's instructions must be observed. The installation properties of wet-applied sealants are described in Section 2.5.

For multi-part materials it is important that the sealant is thoroughly mixed so as to obtain a uniform colour and a consistent cure, and to achieve the intended performance of the sealant. Hand mixing of two-part sealants should be avoided. Mixing is normally by means of a mixer blade fitted to a hand-held electric drill, set to a slow speed (300 to 500 rpm) to avoid heating or aeration of the sealant. Heating from mixing at too high a speed will change the pot life and cure times, aeration could cause bubbling, and both may lead to poor performance, working properties and durability.

Mixer blades are commonly available in a variety of shapes, e.g., horseshoe, spiral, T-bar, triangular. As these vary in efficiency, the sealant supplier should be consulted regarding the most appropriate blade for a given product (this information should normally be included within the mixing instructions).

Whether mixing in the supplied can or another container, it is essential to move the mixer blade around the complete mass of sealant, without entrapping air. For thorough mixing, an efficient procedure is more critical than a long mixing time. Allowing the blade to rotate in a fixed position will not achieve efficient and satisfactory mixing.

Particular attention needs to be given to material at the sides, bottom and corners of the container. Generally, it is necessary to interrupt the process briefly in order to scrape down the sides of the can to ensure that all the sealant is being mixed.

When working in hot conditions, perspiration should not be allowed to contaminate the sealant during mixing – this has been known to have a significant effect on the usable life of some products.

Hand-held drills and mixing blades are convenient, versatile and suitable for most application. However, purpose-made mixing machines may be more suited to some projects, particularly if large batches of viscous products need to be mixed. Such machines can be difficult to move around a site, but they generally provide a high torque at a low speed and give a consistently efficient mixing process.

5.3.8   Sealant application

For most applications on a building envelope gunning of the material is most appropriate. The gun should be capable of maintaining a continuous evacuation pressure on the sealant to avoid entrapment of air in the sealant. If sealant is transferred from larger containers or mixing vessels into cartridges prior to gunning care must be taken to avoid air pockets in the sealant caused by drawing in air during the filling operation. These will interrupt the flow of sealant from the gun and could produce an uneven bead of sealant in the joint.

The most common type of gun is hand-operated, using a pivoted trigger to force a piston down the barrel. Both skeleton (side-bar) and barrel guns are used, the former having the benefit of being lightweight and easy to load with a cartridge.

Pneumatic guns are also available for use with cartridges, flexible sachets (see below) or bulk loading. They can have advantages where there are long runs of uniform joint section with good access. However, the inconvenience imposed by air-lines or portable ('back-pack') compressed-air units generally outweighs the benefits. Extrusion is also more difficult to control in comparison with hand guns, which can be regulated easily by hand-pressure and the rate of operation.

In contrast to adhesives, two-component sealants dispensed from a twin-pack fitted with a static mixing nozzle are not available.

Sealant guns are available with nozzles of different materials and sizes. One-part sealants are frequently used direct from disposable cartridges incorporating plastic nozzles. Site-mixed sealants and sealants supplied in flexible sachets are placed into a reusable cartridge with a replaceable screwed nozzle. Metal nozzles are preferred by some applicators as they do not wear as quickly when abraded by brick and stone. Care should be taken that they do not develop sharp edges that will scratch architectural finishes such as coated aluminium or PVC-U.

Metal nozzles should be chosen to suit the width of the joint. Plastic nozzles should be cut to the correct width, normally at an angle of 45°, to help force the sealant into the joint. For butt joints the nozzle should be slightly narrower than the joint width to avoid placing sealant outside the joint. For fillet joints the nozzle width should ideally be the same as the face width of the fillet.

For very wide joints it may be necessary to fill the joint using several passes of the sealant gun. Sealant should first be placed in the back corners of the joint and successive layers are then built forward to fill the entire joint. To avoid slump in very large joints it may be advisable to let the first layer partly cure before applying further layers. When filling a joint with several beads of sealant care should be taken to avoid the entrapment of air and contaminants such as dust between the beads.

When placing beads of sealant in a joint, the rate of extrusion of the sealant must match the speed at which the gun is moved along the joint. The aim is to produce a continuous, even bead in a single pass that places the correct volume of sealant at all points along the joint. If sealant is extruded too fast for the speed of the gun then too much sealant will be used, the joint will be overfilled, and sealant may be spread onto the surfaces alongside the joint. If the sealant in the joint is too deep it may produce an uneven finish. If the gun is moved too fast for the rate of sealant extrusion then the bead will be too narrow and is unlikely to be even along its length. The finished joint will be too shallow and the cured sealant may be very thin in places. It is also likely that air will be entrapped behind the sealant, reducing adhesion to the joint faces.

5.3.9　Tooling

Tooling of sealants is necessary to compact the sealant into the joint. This ensures full contact between the sealant and the joint face to which it must adhere. It also serves to close any air pockets within the sealant. Tooling of the sealant also provides a neat smooth finish to the sealed joint and a slightly concave surface, which reduces internal stresses resulting from joint movement. Care must be taken to return an adequate depth of sealant (Section 2.8.3). It has been common practice on smaller joints, such as window-to-wall joints, to use the gun nozzle to tool the sealant. This seldom gives proper compaction and adhesion and leads to premature joint failure. Tooling should always be a separate operation from sealant placement.

Tooling of the sealant should be done before the sealant surface cures. Attempts to tool partly cured sealants will distress the placed sealant. For one-part materials that cure from the surface, the skin that forms may be torn from the underlying body of uncured sealant when tooled. The available tooling time for sealants varies from a few minutes for some silicones to several hours for some polysulfides. Care should be taken to place only as much sealant as can be tooled within the tooling time available.

Tooling is normally done with wooden or metal spatulas and similar suitable implements. The tool is often wet with soapy water or detergent to ease movement across the sealant and avoid adhesion. Care should be taken to avoid ingress of water between the sealant and the faces to which it must adhere. Water should be applied to the tool and not the joint and should be used sparingly. The tool should be shaken to remove excess water. Some solutions used to wet tools have been known to discolour light-coloured sealants. For such sealants it is recommended that only water-wet or dry tools are used. Some manufacturers recommend particular tooling solutions.

5.3.10   Protection

Sealing operations should be protected from debris and contamination arising from other site operations. This is necessary during tooling and also during the cure period. Joints should be protected against dust and other contamination until the surface is cured sufficient to prevent adhesion or staining. One-part sealants cure in the presence of air, water or UV; covering of a joint may inhibit curing and any protection used should allow ventilation of the joint.

5.3.11   Cleaning down

Any masking tape should be removed immediately after the tooling of the sealant. This should be done by peeling it across the line of the joint to avoid smearing.

Sealant that has spread or been dropped onto adjacent surfaces should be removed by the sealant manufacturer's recommended methods, if available. Joint cleaners and solvents may be used to clean adjacent surfaces. Care should be taken not to stain or otherwise damage the surface, and the method of cleaning should have been proven at an early stage of the contract on a specimen of the surface or on a small area not readily visible. Removal of sealant, primer and cleaners from porous surfaces can be extremely difficult and proper masking of the surfaces is recommended.

5.3.12   Disposal of materials

Care should be taken in the disposal of excess materials and all cleaning agents and materials, including contaminated cloths. Materials that were hazardous at the time they were brought on to site often remain hazardous after use and the same safety precautions have to be taken for their safe storage after use and disposal.

The sealant applicator should ensure that chemical wastes, spare materials, contaminated solvents, cleaning cloths, etc., are kept separate from more general waste. They should be disposed of safely, in an environmentally acceptable manner. Some sites operate environmental disposal schemes and the sealant applicator will be bound by the site rules for the disposal of waste.

5.3.13   Cleaning of equipment

All brushes used to apply cleaners or primers should be cleaned in accordance with the manufacturer's instructions at regular intervals to avoid contamination of future work. Nozzles, mixing equipment and other tools must be thoroughly cleaned at appropriate periods using suitable cleaning materials during the work to avoid contamination of fresh material. To avoid contamination of one sealant with another, particular attention should be given to cleaning guns and nozzles when they are to be used with a different generic type of sealant.

5.4 SITE ADHESION TESTS

There are no standard tests for the adhesion or strength of installed sealant. Non-destructive testing is carried out by pressing the sealant and looking for consistent behaviour at different points along the joint. This may give information about the depth of sealant. It will also reveal any serious lack of adhesion if the sealant separates cleanly away from the joint face.

Greater information is obtained by cutting out a short length of the sealant from the joint. This will show the depth of the sealant in the joint, the presence of voids, poor mixing or cure. Tearing a length of sealant from the joint will indicate whether it has properly wet out the joint surface and adhered as required. When the sealant is pulled from the joint the tear should go through the sealant, leaving a residual layer of sealant bonded to the joint surface. This indicates a cohesive failure of the material. If the sealant peels directly away from the joint surface then an adhesive failure has occurred and the sealant has not bonded properly.

Any suspect lengths of joint should be considered in the light of the records available of the sequence of work, operatives used, weather conditions, temperature, and batches of material used. Further sections of sealant should then be cut out and examined.

5.5 REPAIR AND RESEALING

5.5.1 Repair

Defects discovered after the joint has been sealed should normally be cut out and resealed. Sealant may be either cut back or fully removed. It may be acceptable to make good surface defects by cutting back the outer layer of sealant and applying new sealant to the joint. Remedial work is always a difficult issue and the extent and nature of the remedial work will be the subject of discussion between the sealant applicator, the contractor, the client and their advisers. The sealant manufacturer should be consulted at an early stage concerning suitable methods for the remedial work.

If a joint sealant is cut back and a new sealant placed over the original material, the sealants must be of the same brand. The manufacturer should be consulted and only sealants that will bond to cured sealant should be used in this way.

5.5.2 Resealing

Joints suffering from inadequate sealant depth, poor bond to the joint faces, or inconsistent mixing of the sealant can be repaired only by cutting out the sealant entirely and resealing the joint. The cause of the failure should be established and the sealing method adapted to prevent a second failure. The joint should be cleaned and prepared as if the work was an initial sealing operation. Some sealants can be applied to surfaces on which a residue of original sealant is still attached. For most sealants it will be necessary to remove the original sealant completely, clean the joint interfaces and reprime the surfaces. If the remedial work arises from an adhesive failure of the sealant then it will be necessary to clean and reprime the joint surfaces, whichever sealant is being used. Further guidance on resealing is given in Section 2.11.

Bibliography

AAMA 501-94 Methods of Test for Exterior Walls, 1994

ACI 504R-77 Guide to Joint Sealants for Concrete Structures, ACI Manual of Concrete Practice, 1977

Aluminium Window Association: The Use of Mastics and Sealants on Site, Edition 1, undated

BASA: 1988 Safe Handling of Adhesives and Sealants in Industry: a guide for users and safety officers

BCSA/SCI 203/91 National Structural Steelwork Specification for Building Structures. Second edition

BPF: 1993 Gaskets and Weatherstrips for Windows, Doors and Curtain Walling

BRE Digest 137: 1972 Principles of Joint Design

BRE Digest 199: 1977 Getting Good Fit

BRE Digest 223: 1979 Wall Cladding: Designing to Minimise Defects due to Inaccuracies and Movements

BRE Digest 227: 1979 Estimation of Thermal and Moisture Movements and Stresses: Pt 1

BRE Digest 228: 1979 Estimation of Thermal and Moisture Movements and Stresses: Pt 2

BRE Digest 229: 1979 Estimation of Thermal and Moisture Movements and Stresses: Pt 3

BRE Digest 234: 1980 Accuracy in Setting-out

BRS CP 1/71: 1971 Joints in the Context of an Assembly Process

BRS CP 2/71: 1971 The Extent and Rate of Joint Movement in Modern Buildings

BRS CP 5/71: 1971 The Relationship between Component Size and Joint Dimension

BRS CP 10/73: 1973 Width Variation of Cladding

BRS CP 86/74: 1974 Window to Wall Joints

BS476: Fire Tests on Building Materials and Structures (31 parts)

BS1192: Pt 1: 1984 Construction Drawing Practice. Recommendations for general principles

BS1217: 1986 Specification for Cast Stone

BS3712: Pt 1: 1991 Building and Construction Sealants. Methods of test for homogeneity, relative density and penetration

BS3712: Pt 2: 1973 Building and Construction Sealants. Methods of test for seepage, staining, shrinkage, shelf life and paintability

BS3712: Pt 3: 1974 Building and Construction Sealants. Methods of test for application life, skinning properties and tack-free time

BS3712: Pt 4: 1991 Building and Construction Sealants. Method of test for adhesion in peel

BS4254: 1983 Specification for Two-part Polysulfide-based Sealants

BS4255: Pt 1: 1986 Rubber used in Preformed Gaskets for Weather Exclusion from Buildings. Specification for Non-cellular Gaskets

BS4873: 1986 Specification for Aluminium Alloy Windows

BS5215: 1986 Specification for One-part Gun Grade Polysulfide-based Sealants

BS5390: 1976 Code of Practice for Stone Masonry

BS5493: 1977 Code of Practice for Protective Coating of Iron and Steel Structures again Corrosion

BS5606: 1990 Guide to Accuracy in Building

BS5628: Code of Practice for Use of Masonry (3 parts)

BS5889: 1989 Specification for One-part Gun Grade Silicone-based Sealants

BS6093: 1993 Code of Practice for Design of Joints and Jointing in Building Construction

BS6100 Glossary of Building and Civil Engineering Terms (several parts)

BS6213: 1982 Guide to Selection of Constructional Sealants

BS6262: 1982 Code of Practice for Glazing in Buildings

BS6375: Pt 1: 1989 Performance of Windows. Classification for weathertightness (including guidance on selection and specification)

BS6954: Pt 3: 1988 Tolerances for Building. Recommendations for Selecting Target Size and Predicting Fit

BS6750: 1986 Specification for Modular Co-ordination in Building

BS7307: 1990 Method for Presentation of Dimensional Accuracy Data in Building Construction. Building Tolerances. Measurement of Buildings and Building Products

BS7412: 1991 Specification for Plastic Windows made from PVC-U Extruded Hollow Profiles

BS7543: 1992 Guide to Durability of Buildings and Building Elements, Products and Components

BS8110: Pt 1: 1997 Structural Use of Concrete. Code of Practice for Design and Construction

BS8110: Pt 2: 1985 Structural Use of Concrete. Code of Practice for Special Circumstances

BS8200: 1985 Code of Practice for Design of Non-loadbearing External Vertical Enclosures of Buildings

BS8210: 1986 Guide to Building Maintenance Management

BS8213: Pt 4: 1990 Windows, Doors and Rooflights. Code of Practice for the Installation of Replacement Windows and Doorsets in Dwellings

BS8297: 1995 Code of Practice for Design and Installation of Non-loadbearing Precast Concrete Cladding

BS8298: 1994 Code of Practice for Design and Installation of Natural Stone Cladding and Lining

BS EN 28339: 1991 Building Construction. Jointing products. Sealants. Determination of Tensile Properties

BS EN 28340: 1991 Building Construction. Jointing Products. Sealants. Determination of Tensile Properties at Maintained Extension

BS EN ISO 9000: 1994 Quality Management and Quality Assurance Standards

BS ISO 10563: 1991 Building Construction. Sealants for Joints. Determination of Change in Mass and Volume

BS ISO 10590: 1991 Building construction. Sealants. Determination of Adhesion/Cohesion Properties at Maintained Extension after Immersion in Water

BS ISO 10591: 1991 Building Construction. Sealants. Determination of Adhesion/Cohesion Properties after Immersion in Water

BS ISO 11431: 1993 Building Construction. Sealants. Determination of Adhesion/Cohesion Properties after Exposure to Artificial Light through Glass

BS ISO 11432: 1993 Building Construction. Sealants. Determination of Resistance to Compression

BS ISO 11600: 1993 Building Construction. Sealants. Classification and Requirements

CIRIA PR16: 1995 Paints and Coatings, Adhesives and Sealants – Volume F

CIRIA Report 125: 1993 A Guide to the Control of Substances Hazardous to Health in Construction

CIRIA Report 145: 1995 CDM Regulations – Case Study Guidance for Designers: an Interim Report

CIRIA SP44: 1986 Movement and Cracking in Long Masonry Walls

CIRIA SP80: 1991 Manual of Good Practice in Sealant Application

CIRIA SP87: 1992 Wall Technology

CIRIA SP90: 1992 Site Safety Handbook

CIRIA SP116: 1995 Environmental Impact of Materials, Volume A – Summary

CIRIA Technical Note 107: 1981 Design for Movement in Buildings, Alexander S J and Lawson R

CIRIA Technical Note 113: 1983 A Suggested Design Procedure for Accuracy in Building

CWCT: 1996 The Performance of Gaskets in Window and Cladding Systems – a 'State of the Art' Review

CWCT: 1996 Standard for Curtain Walling

ISO 2445: 1972 Joints in Buildings: Fundamental Principles for Design

ISO 3447: 1975 Joints in Buildings: General Check-list of Joint Functions

ISO 6927: 1991 Sealants Vocabulary

ISE, Designing for Building Movements, Proceedings of seminar held at Institution of Structural Engineers, Dublin, 20 May 1994

BEECH, J C (1985)
Test Methods for the Movement Capability of Building Sealants: the State of the Art
Riley Materials and Structures, Vol. 18, No. 108, pp 473–82

BEECH, J C and AUBREY, D W (1987)
Joint Primers and Sealants: Performance between Porous Cladding
BRE Information Paper, 9/87

BONSHOR, R B and ELDRIDGE, L L (1974)
Graphical Aids for Tolerances and Fits: Handbook for Manufacturers, Designers and Builders, Building Research Establishment Report

DAMUSIS, A (ed.) (1967)
Sealants
Reinhold Publishing Corporation

FELDMAN, D (1989)
Polymeric Building Materials
Elsevier Applied Science

GJELSVIK, T, BERG, S B and JOHANSEN, T S (1987)
Building Sealants
Norwegian Building Research Institute, *Report 30*

KLOSOWSKI, J M (1989)
Sealants in Construction
Marcel Dekker Inc

LACASSE, M, THOMAS, J R and WOOLSEY, L G (1994)
Sealant Joint Design, Selection and Specification using Knowledge-based System
Software. Proceedings of the International Conference on Building Envelope Systems
and Technology

MARTIN, B (1977)
Joints in Buildings
George Godwin

MORTON, J (1988)
Designing for Movement in Brickwork
BDA Design, Note 10

MYERS, J C (1990a)
Sealant Configurations and Performance
Architectural Record January

MYERS, J C (1990b)
Behaviour of Fillet Sealant Joints
Building sealants: materials, properties and performance (T F O'Connor, ed.) ASTM
STP 1069

ORAM, W R (1978)
Pre-cast Concrete Cladding
Cement and Concrete Association

PANEK, J R and COOK, J P (1984)
Construction Sealants and Adhesives, 2nd edition
John Wiley & Sons

WOLF, A T (1990)
Studies of the Ageing Behaviour of Gun-grade Building Joint Sealants – the State of
the Art
Riley Materials and Structures, Vol. 23, pp. 142–52

WOLF, A T (1991)
Movement Capability of Sealants
Construction and Building Materials, Vol. 5, No. 3, September, pp. 127–34

WOOLMAN, R (1987)
Sealants in Modern Buildings
Surveyors Publications

WOOLMAN, R and HUTCHINSON, A (1994)
Resealing of Buildings – a Guide to Good Practice
Butterworth Heinemann